World is My Best Teacher

*

Dedicate this Book to all Youth of the World who are Seeking Success

*

Special Thanks to Young Reader who See this Book as:

"A Book that Simplifies Success. Thought Provoking Easy to Understand & for all ages. Definitely a Smart Right Choice to Read".

Koreen. R

# INDEX

# INTRODUCTION

"Nail Your Success" a practical book or in precise words; first three steps analysis and next three steps execution book, to achieve your target, goal, mission, top results and ultimately become top achievers, guaranteed to reach your destiny in any field of life; Business, Athlete, Job Executive, Art, Adventure and Lifestyle etc.

Our dream, vision, aim, target, drives us through multiple choices and inspirations we have from this world, we need to carefully pick "the best one small smart choice" to "nail success", people who have picked up wrong choices are the one who spend most time in prison, longer the prison life, worst the choice was picked, we reached from biological tribal life 1.0, to technological life 3.0 stepping on moon and further by picking up right smart choices. Always place that small smart choice under microscope "narrow your focus & seek the truth" to unfold its characteristics, so that you may not fall into trap of biased likes or dislikes, further work on it to find out how much effort, comfort, money, health and time you can spend on it to get reward through "80/20 principle", otherwise you may quit in middle. "Be proactive, make yourself 100% responsible" on your work and complete it, selecting a high performer team is also your 100% responsibility if people working for you, healthy life make us proactive. "Line up activities for yourself and for your team & remove distractions", after all; entire management sciences studies tell us same at the end that, "break segments into last individual independent entity; line them in a sequence ready to be performed in a process already defined". Keep on running the process, keeping in mind "compound effect" formula and accelerate. Success is not luck; luck has almost zero probability proved in last chapter by mathematics. Success is a sequence of right steps & choices.

Almost all books talks in general and give different success rules / thumbs / secrets / keys, I was looking for practical approaches other than, time keeping, motivation, planning, strategy, integrity, faith etc. which we all should have by default, my curiosity increased that what are the steps or tools taken by successful people to "nail their successes". I studied long and seen practically and discovered astonishing factors of success, so I decided to write Book to benefit others so that this planet becomes the Planet of "success nailers". One thing is important and linked with success is; healthy life. Postpones or Laziness instead of Pro Active life cannot let us succeed no matter how much budget we have with lots of ideas. It is never too late for any of us to achieve anything at any stage. There are thousands of examples who achieved extraordinary at later stage, for example on 14 October 2016 Grand Mother Bettie Butler of Marion in Indiana celebrated her 95th Birthday by skydiving from 13000 feet in the air as 40 of her closet friends and family watched her from the Ground {1}. It takes lot of courage mental as well as preparation, physical health to nail it, It is the matter of when you visualize, make aim to achieve certain thing, this book will guide you through in;

"Nailing your Success".

# ONE SMALL & SMART CHOICE

Always start with one small thing at a time that should be a Smart choice.

What is Life? The way we spend our time through Choices we selected in our past till the moment ago is called life or one's life time collection of choices is equal to his / her life.

"We are the best creatures on this plant so our choices have to be the best in our life."

We all keep on working this question throughout our life; what to do each moment of life? Then we think of a few options, select one, selected one option is in fact a choice. We all live on choices we have available in our surroundings in this entire life every single moment, a human being is capable to pick up any of the choice with some restriction of law of nature and values. Never go against norms and values, animals don't have values, by hook or crook they attack on their prey. All religions teach morality and norms. So go for those choices which are hygienic healthy and not against the laws.

Constantly, consciously or unconsciously every single moment we are comparing choices and selecting those which suits to us. Selecting a choice is in fact selecting a direction towards destiny of big or small aim, keep it as an analysis stage for the time being till couple of few more checks and balances, till 80/20 analysis coming next which will determine either to finally adopt it as an authentic choice before start investing money, time, health otherwise recovery will be costly, so it is very important to select the best choice & take one smart small step at a time.

"Small is Beautiful & Powerful" Jack Ma founder alibaba.com

Today's time is Technology advancement era life 3.0 with full of innovations developmental, surprises every day, Previous era was life 2.0 a cultural time period; formation of tribes, customs, societies and before that life 1.0 a simple biological human, whose main aim was to just survive from tough environment {1}; When human searched for food very first time in history, at that time human curiously eaten some plants or other substances which were not in knowledge of humans of its poison's effects. Many people could have died because no pre-knowledge of presence of poison, once it's consequences experienced then message spread across person to person that this plant or substance not to eat. Slowly human moved towards better choices better food. Names were declared to plants and substances; still we have different names of same item in different geographic locations. We reached this stage by picking up right choices gradually, available in our environment all the time. It is a long history of human, learned from bad choices of war, illness, facing tough weathers, learned how to protect humanity. Before the invention of fire, animals use to attack human during sleep, fire made animals scared and kept distance, fire cooked food and killed germs, fire made tools, fire helped grow population very fast. Many choices appeared with the help of fire, which helped human in spending quality of life & growth. Since the invention of fire industrial revolution took its land mark astonishing role, which is surprising us even today by producing innovative products and job creations in different sectors.

Life 1.0 to Life 3.0 in Pictures. Ancient human to Astronaut on Moon.

Ane Ancient Human to Astronaut Man on Moon by adopting smart small choices

One of the examples and evidence of picking up best choice surprised me that heavy loaders or cargo trucks, trails maximum uploaded weight is limited to truck or trails excel power. We came to this conclusion or rule by picking up right choice and learned from cause of the accidents or damage to vehicle or damage to the roads as well. Those who picked up wrong choices suffered from it and caused accidents, created suffering for others too, people in prisons are the example of picking up wrong choices. Longer the prison life is, worse the choice was picked by that individual.

To avoid picking wrong choices; laws are made. Criminal laws to control crime for a calm peaceful society, commercial laws to control business disputes, traffic laws to protect us from accidents, sports laws for each game to have fair play and human rights to protect people from abuse of power etc. all laws are made by analyzing the best possible remedy and punishment for those who picked up wrong choices. We moved from biological life to artificial intelligence life by picking up right & the best choices. Rules & standards are made when best results and optimizations are achieved, standards are set, and this is how we have moved this far in the shape of developed societies, best systems in place in all sort of sectors of life.

We all have choices, our life is full of choices around us, from the very first step taken by a toddler of its life, that baby start picking up choices from that stage, baby move towards whatever attracts, which may not be rational but time teaches baby as it grows, what is a good choice or bad a choice was. We pick for example lamb to cook, at the same time we also have a choice to make lentil soup or fry a fish, all in our control to fill our hunger, stay healthy or even fit to perform certain sports. Same as this, all matters of life we deal in, we deal with the choices we have, which can be right or wrong. We will figure out at the end of this book that this is a complete cycle from picking up a one small smart choice to a successful result, we have very important role of taking first step right then next right and so on. We were not having such knowledge, skills and power before as compare to today's variety of developments in all fields of life, like; medicine, chemical, electronic, mechanical, agricultural developments, space sciences etc. to reach here it took us millions of years. This success is not sudden. It is a long struggle in perspective of entire civilizations. We are all the time fighting tug of war among choices, likes, dreams, different ideas, solutions, approaches to handle a matter etc. one after another throughout life. Best approach is to handle it by not using force like we use in tug of war, instead look into its merits and demerits then drag it toward you by using three execution steps mentioned in this book for clear guaranteed success.

One small activity at one time very important to understand because our brain works in a certain way that do not support multi-tasking, there was a time when organizations were looking for hiring people who are performing multitasking, may be to save cost. How many incidents we read in newspapers of deaths from driving while listening phone, road crossing while listening phone etc., below are the causes, and very important to understand how our brain works, because we rely on 100% on our brains to perform every single task, smallest to big, simplest to complex, shortest to longest.

Our learning and how our brain works are very important to understand that a neural network in simple language is a group of interconnected neurons as many as stars in our galaxy that are able to influence each other's behaviors. These neurons are connected via junction of average 1000 neurons called synapses. These 100 trillion synapses connections that encode most of the information in our brain. Each neuron updates its state, time, steps by simply averaging together the inputs from all connected neurons, weighting them by the synaptic strengths optionally adding a constant and then applying that's called an activation function to the results to compute its next state {2}. Disruption in between one activity affects, stops process and immediately starts working on other activity, again disruption, then again effect on ongoing process resulting loss of concentration and stress on synapses, this process is very fast. Computer CPU looks like doing multitasking but it's an illusion. CPU works under sequence of well-organized commands being performed, one task at a time and mostly back forth so fast that it looks like doing multitasking but in fact performing one activity at a time. Multitasking create stress on neurons. When a music drummer beating drums and plates to create music looks like doing multiple hitting and multitasking but repeat it in slow motion, see hitting one object at one time and move back forth so fast becomes an illusion.

Starting from big is very risky, may be you can lose entire capital if invested all simultaneously or jump from K2 will kill immediately, all climbers go up and come down by very carefully taking one step at a time after acclimatizing in few days.

One of the greatest example supporting and giving evidence to my point is my ex company Ericsson, an innovator and constant development through Research & Development, that has changed the entire world in the field of Telecom industry, which enabled all industries and people from all ages to easy access of communication, instant delivery of message, which includes voice, text and video globally and into space.

My working experience for almost a decade with Ericsson; a Swedish Telecom Company; that was founded in 1876 by Lars Magnus Ericsson. He did not achieve this success in a single day; it is a constant struggle from 1876 to 2019. We are enjoying the benefits of this revolution today. No one knew in 1876 that we will have video conference live and we will watch TV live on phone and billions of dollars commercial activities in place on mobile phones, computers with the help of internet, like amazon.com & alibaba.com. What they did is; one small scope of work analyzed then created a product one after another, not in a single day big scope and telecom industry is developed, it is the constant working on small steps which collectively shaped Ericsson a turnkey solution provider of state-of-the-art communication system to the entire world. Now a day's latest development of 5G internet service and product will enable mobiles to communicate directly with other machines, machines will be free from human brain's direct control on them and will function own its own, what we have to do is to set limits for machines that can function to certain level free from human intervention. May be in some situations we will allow 100% autonomy to machines, for example to perform operations. We will see such machines soon. Machines will share their statistics to learn from each other and improve their procedures.

Ericsson founder below is the man who made this planet very efficient through magical development day by day in telecom revolution and its effects and benefits are far away to other planets in the shape of radars and radio waves, which helps two ways traffic of data in the shape of for example; images from mars, communication with international space station etc. He did not achieve all on very first day, one step by step gradually made it possible.

| | |
|---|---|
| Born | 5 May 1846 Värmskog, Värmland, Sweden–Norway |
| Died | 17 December 1926 (aged 80) Hågelby gård, Botkyrka |
| Nationality | Swedish |
| Occupation | Inventor, entrepreneur |
| Known for | Founder of telephone equipment manufacturer Ericsson |

Lars Magnus Ericsson at the age of 20, who came from a farmer family, he moved to Stockholm in 1867; He then worked for six years for an instrument maker named Ollers & Co. who mainly created telegraph equipment. Because of his skills, he was given two state scholarships to study instrument making abroad between 1872 and 1875, he constructed Sweden's first telephone line at the age of 17, his company later expanded to world's 180 countries, more than 95000 people working. Ericsson had 35% market share globally in 2012 in 2G/3G/4G Mobile network infrastructures. Revenue in 2018 was 210.8 Billion SEK. How Ericsson reached so far? starting from smart small one thing at a time, moved on to next best choice of fixed lines, broadband, GSM, IP, managed services, value added services and multimedia is incredible journey {3}.

Ericsson still leading the world of telecom, such a powerful tool mix of hardware and software (mechanical + electrical) has been developed, distances and time delays have been eliminated. Data travel has become so fast that with a glimpse of an eye reaches around the world and even to other planets too.

Different types of planes, helicopters, rockets to other planets, fighter gets we see are not built in few days. First attempt to make a plane by two brother's individual idea has progressed and has become a full-fledged industry in a century, collectively a very sophisticated, complex, safe, fast and reliable aviation industry now that a single human cannot gain entire knowledge. In hundred years step by step we reached this stage. First flying machine had below parameters;

Glider vital statistics {4}

"Just the Facts." Wright Brothers Aero plane Company. Retrieved: April 18, 2012

https://en.wikipedia.org/wiki/Wright_brothers

| Year | Wingspan | Wing area | Chord | Camber | Aspect Ra | Length | Weight |
|---|---|---|---|---|---|---|---|
| 1900 | 17.5 ft | 165 sq ft | 5 ft | 1.0/20 | 3:05:01 | 11.5 ft | 24 kg |
| 1901 | 22 ft | 290 sq ft | 7 ft | 1/12-1/19 | 3:01 | 14 ft | 44 kg |
| 1902 | 32 ft | 305 sq ft | 5 ft | 1/2-1/24 | 6:05:01 | 17 ft | 51 kg |

(This airfoil caused severe stability problems; the Wrights modified the camber on-site.)

First flight of the Wright Flyer, December 17, 1903, Orville piloting, Wilbur running at wingtip    https://en.wikipedia.org/wiki/Wright_brothers

Then with better choices; made biggest commercial plane, they were not aware in 1903 that one day Air Bus A380 can lift around 555 passengers, which is not possible to land take off on all air ports or runways in the world due to its size. Step by step gradually aviation industry improved, reached & achieved below capability;

**Airbus A380 Spec Table General**

| **Typical Seating** | **555 passengers** |
| --- | --- |
| Maximum Zero Fuel Weight | 361,000kg (795869lb) |
| Maximum Fuel Capacity | 320,000 Liters |
| Typical Operating Empty Weight | 277,000kg (610,700lb) |

An A380-800 of Emirates the largest operator of the aircraft

It was first delivered to Singapore Airlines on 15 October 2007 and entered service on 25 October {5}.

[6] "Commercial Aircraft Airbus and Emirates reach agreement on A380 fleet, sign new wide body orders" (Press release). Airbus. 14 February 2019.

Then on 13 April 2019 Stratolaunch System Corp built and its first flight of world's largest plane measured by its wing span at space port California,  reaching 15,000 ft. (4,600 m) and 165kn (305km/h) in a 2 h 29 min flight

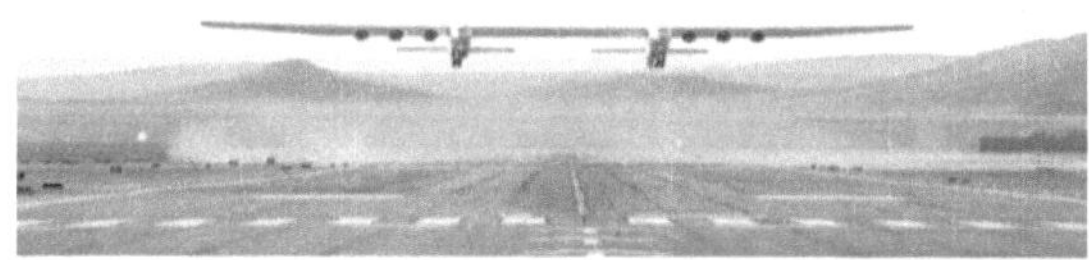

{6} https://spacenews.com/stratolaunch-plane-makes-first-flight/  Wikipedia Stratolaunch becomes world's largest aircraft to fly". Flight global. April 13, 2019

This all journey became possible due to started from one small and smart choice to big smart choice that state of the art machines built in almost 100 years' time period. Further steps which helped reaching this extraordinary development will be explained in next chapters one by one, but to reach this level how important is to select first step of success ladder, that from now onward we can make an un-imaginable flying machines-like drones, rockets, space crafts.

It is all possible due to converting of ideas visions into choices we have to make it happen; drone taxi drone ambulance drone pizza delivery flying car machines are examples of it. This all happened due to Wright Brother's individual vision became the collective vision of aviation's industry, then moved to space technology's vision at large that now it has become one of the biggest industries around the world. Because it has become such a wide scope that it has reached beyond the individual capacity, now only small visions aims choices can and add value to its presence from individual level, it has become impossible to get all knowledge in one brain. We collectively now taking it to next level through research and development.

Facebook was basically the idea of Harvard college students and roommates Mark Zuckerberg, Eduardo Saverin, Andrew McCollum, Dustin Moskovitz, and Chris Hughes who developed online social media networking. Initially the idea was just to connect Harvard students, later it became global social media connection tool, now it reached one of the top Billions commercial entity.

Think big but always start small and smart one thing at a time. Sometimes even big picture is not captured or initiated initially as in the case of Facebook, it was just the idea to connect only Harvard students but exploring more choices makes it bigger at later stage that billions of dollars economy is being run on this single plat-form.

Sabeer Bhatia landed in America with only $250 in his pocket, he had big plans in his mind to start something, which can grow as never happened in history, his choice was the smartest choice, he started from small one thing, made Hotmail, and Microsoft watched its growth and eventually bought it for $400 million {7}. Success is not just one step of thinking big, start from one smart small choice; it has few more steps in coming chapters to guarantee a success. Sabeer Bhatia could not have achieved this without following next steps.

Most of the big food chain stores, supermarkets started from single store, these are all grown from small to big, growth mindset is very important to achieve this level. Do not fear; follow all success cycle steps. Only fear for the waste of time.

Think new. Future top Billions company or product will be from something which do not exist before, as PayPal co-founder Peter Thiel wrote in his book Zero to One, the next Bill Gates will not build an operating system, the next Larry Page or Sergy Brin would not make a search engine. If you are copying these guys, you are not learning from them. It is very easy to duplicate or replicate a model, if we do so we will take the world from 1 to n than making something fresh and new, success is in 0 to1 choice. All these people taken one smart small step and gained very big, resulted; dominated and marked its impact on us.

Amazon founder Jeff Bezos divorce leaves world's richest man on 4th April 2019 with 75% of couple's Amazon stock to half of its size, Mackenzie Bezos receives estimated $36 Billion, which means Mackenzie moved to top Couple of world's richest women. The world's richest woman, according to Bloomberg estimates, is the L'Oreal cosmetics heiress Françoise Bettencourt Meyers, whose net worth is estimated at $45.6 Billion {8}. I leave analysis for the readers to decide who out of the two; Jeff Bezos & Mackenzie Bezos taken right or wrong first step, when they marry.

K2 is 28251 Feet high, to reach top 1st small step one at a time out of almost 28251 steps and 6 choices as shown in below picture very important to understand, otherwise you may get loss in extreme cold, low oxygen. Same as our life is, for any activity; looking for a job, going for a relation, making a holidays plan, purchasing any item, speaking few words we do have choices located around us, we just need to figure out, which choice is the best. Life is only a single choice and cannot come back and restart from same location. If God keeps us alive, we return to start point again, meanwhile we would have lost that time, resources, energy etc. life do not give second chance if bad choice is selected, and high price has to pay.

1st step is actually practical start towards your aim, vision, goal tc

K2 six different routes, Mountaineers make one choice from the available 6; A, B, C, D, E, F according to weather and

snow conditions. Diverting from a choice and mixing c & f route can take life, choice has to be right at initial stage of taking very first step.

When a choice is being picked, compare it with other options available, look for alternatives. Sometimes alternative give better options, can be cost effective, can save time, more efficient and can reduce efforts. Always go for alternates and substitutes, after comparisons still think original choice is the best then go for it. Undoing it at later stage means picked up choice was not correct, Berlin wall built between East Germany and West Germany was not the good option, because after fifty-eight years it has to be demolished. People suffered too, one side of Germany was developed and other side left behind underdeveloped. Later it became one Germany eventually. Building a wall was terrible choice. Always think about K2 has six routes before taking any step-in life, choose the best from different alternatives. In my life I always paid extra price, when I did not look for alternatives. When I looked back, I found out I was in hurry and not looked for other options or substitutes, which were short, cost effective.

If your aim is to do PhD in space sciences, that student must study Physics and Math in early classes, without understanding of both subjects in early classes cannot complete PhD in space sciences. So choice has to be right to complete big picture.

Selected choice at this stage is not giving 100% assurance of success but it's a first step towards it, choice can be dropped if at the stage of 80/20 principle result came out as less productive choice or some other option is more fruitful. Because we all have likes dislikes, desires may or may not be productive, and the only way to check it is at least through narrowing down your focus and seek the truth, plus how much effort can we make to get this reward through 80/20 effect principle.

To have a clear authentic choice we must have clear objectives. Clear objectives are of different nature's, long term objectives; such as career seeking, aim to have a home in Beverly hill, medium term objectives; holidays plan in a year and short term objectives; daily routine life matters. To achieve all above objectives, we have to start somewhere i.e. work on choices we have. For a dream home first of all need to work on present financial situation. Figure out gap of what you have and what you don't have to get that dream house, how to cover that gap? Now you need to work on choices you have. Work out how much time required completing this gap. Choice A can be to do over time according to your situations, second job, or quit a job, start small business, change a job, mortgage, before picking up a choice it is very important not pick up un-rational choice. Where matters are of large money are involved or matter of strategic importance, these are the decisions whose impact is large, must be taken after careful vigilance and after working on different options available, take time, which require to put it through different test coming in next chapters, like reaching top of K2 is a matter of strategic importance, long before preparation is required, physical fitness, endurance etc. under such cold weather low oxygen, you cannot simple follow your desire and start climbing. Fittest people reach top.

Medium term objectives also require same working, taking an expedition? do some research where you want to go, weather, foods available, places to go, accommodations, travel ease etc.

Daily routine matters require quick decisions; do not consider them of less importance, less impact on our life. This is not rational, give them importance too and make a habit of putting everything on scale of seeking the truth by putting it under microscope and narrowing down your focus towards this choice, then put it under 80/20 principle. Both test will tell you plus minus then easy to make decision. Your practice can make you fast accurate decision maker that even walking on the road, dozens of analyses can be done in one go. Try to turn this into your habit, that before going for a choice make above two tests, you will change your life.

Strong purpose make you prepare to pick up strong choice, picking up weak choice for strong purpose will definitely drop you half the way. There is a difference between strong purpose and strong emotions. Strong emotions do not let us see clear picture, so very important to seek the truth. Emotions play vital role in covering up the actual reality, strong feeling driving one's circumstances, which may not be productive, our mood can divert us from reality. It is also a mental state with nervous system brought on by chemical changes variously associated with thoughts feeling behavioral responses and a degree of pleasure or displeasure.

The most important factor in achieving success is to align your choices with your purpose one at a time. Clarity of thoughts reflects in your selecting a choice. Clarity of thoughts gives you clear purpose. Work on clarity seeks the truth rather working on desires directly. Bring your desire on the table of microscope. Your desire should reflect in clear small smart choice one at a time and further it should go into your purpose of life. Once to have this sequence you will move forward from here faster to faster with clear direction and execution on any matter associated to it.

Do not create a zigzag crossing purpose with choice as shown in below picture;

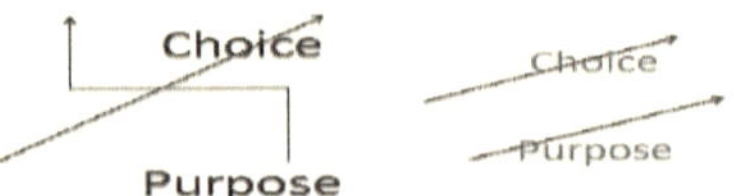


De tracking will cost high; loss of energy, time, resources etc. let's suppose a train destination is from Copenhagen to Stockholm "amazing journey of my life" and we take train to unknown destination, can we reach on time on same ticket? Answer is no, same as the situations are with choices, we take every day for some purposes. Some time we feel 'aah wonderful' it is when we are aligned with choice vs purpose, and when we say 'what the hell' means we are not on track. The biggest battle going on every single moment through our ears eyes continuously keep on feeding us with choices, our rational approach described can tell us to adopt this choice and ignore other one.

Emotions can be defined as a positive or negative experience that are associated with a particular pattern of physiological activity." Emotions produce different physiological, behavioral and cognitive changes. The original role of emotions was to motivate adaptive behaviors that in the past would have contributed to the passing on of genes through survival, reproduction, and kin selection {9}. So emotions should not occupy heavily on reality, purpose has to be legitimate, ethical, rewarding or business idea, feasibility in our favor. Positive emotions should be used as tool to reach destiny.

The best way to work on choices is to write it down, writing down helps absorb its effects and automatically does self-analysis. Writing down choices will automatically help you identify top few choices.

Selected choice must be backed by some knowledge. Little knowledge can be extended by research, discussion with experts, self-reading, and never ever hesitate taking help from others & professionals. On few occasions I lost huge amount of money and time too on just self-assumptions and not extended my knowledge to level of expertise have it.

The greatest gift of God to humans is freedom to choose. Every human is equal to a product in the result of all the choices we have made so far. Mother Teresa; Mary Teresa Bojaxhiu, commonly known as Mother Teresa and honored in the Roman Catholic Church as Saint Teresa of Calcutta, was an Albanian-Indian Roman Catholic nun and missionary. In 1950, Teresa founded the Missionaries of Charity, a Roman Catholic religious congregation that had over 4,500 nuns and was active in 133 countries in 2012. The congregation manages homes for people who are dying of HIV/AIDS, leprosy and tuberculosis, when our society was rejecting those who are victims of these diseases. It also runs soup kitchens, dispensaries, mobile clinics, children's and family counseling programs, as well as orphanages and schools. Members take vows of chastity, poverty, and obedience, and also profess a fourth vow—to give "wholehearted free service to the poorest of the poor {10}. She received 1962 Ramon Magsaysay Peace Prize and 1979 Nobel Peace prize. Her life was full of humanity working for others to end their suffering. She picked up such choices that she became mother of hundreds of thousand's people.

We make our fate by picking up right choices.

Life is all about making the Right Choices.

# NARROW YOUR FOCUS & SEEK THE TRUTH

Never start or adopt a choice without seeking the truth or without narrowing down your focus to it. What is a focus? Means putting down selected choice under micro scope.

Micro scope narrows down focus to solve the question; either it is ameba cell or cancer cell. Questions help identifying the answers. Always write down questions and keep writing their answers until you find right answer about any matter, especially matters of higher stakes of financial importance and matters of strategic importance. Success nailers always look for opportunities and frequently take help from others, do research, ask questions until they get best answer or solution. Even if professionals need to hire, get them on board to unfold the facts. This is in fact digging down and seeking the truth by narrowing down the focus. Never ever act straight or do straight investment, spend time and health on the choice of your desire or in case someone told you, until you seek the truth, otherwise you may fall into trap, where no return path to go back to your original time or at your original financial position in case of failure.

Narrow your focus & seek the truth means get the complete knowledge of the product, idea, process, people and action you are going to take. Prior knowledge does not necessarily exist with us, if we are attracted by the certain choice, people learn, and then look for alternates or get expert opinions.

Following two birds at the same time will make you lose sight from both of them. I am an occasional hunter so know this rule by practice. Remember one small smart choice at a time.

We will discuss here the same single selected best smart choice among many available as mentioned in previous chapter to further analyses its credibility, authenticity, usefulness, rewarding and meeting objectives. Because not every choice can be perfect, need to dig out truth. Selecting a best choice even though with very care does not mean a guarantee to success. Success is still few steps away, success is on 7th step. At any stage before kickoff, choice can be dropped, if not passed the go ahead test, one more analysis step from here.

We are seeking the truth; it will unfold its characteristics. Many of us some time select a choice forced by our emotions and forced by our biased behaviors of personal likes and dislikes, towards that product, investment, choice, not by its merits or demerits. Many of us are attracted by speculations, away from the actual position and reality of the facts. Speculation some time deliberately spread by people at back of the scene to gain hidden objectives. They play it very tactfully after lot of working. Desires and emotions dominate facts and provide cover up to its true pictures. Relations based upon desires and emotions also provide cover ups, identifying true feature and identifying true characteristics is possible by narrowing down your focus, It's characteristics must be written down in a list, make category of top to bottom, give them numbering based on its value or weight both positive and negative aspects, then make decision, either to live with this one negative aspect or not comprisable, for example many people snore during sleep, up to you to ignore but if someone is a liar that is not ignorable.

Let's suppose you own a shop of antique products in the middle of very hustle and bustle area of Las Vegas, you buy and sell artifacts. One day a guy sold you pretty old coins on a reasonably good price, you could make good margin in an auction online. Next time he brings a coin very old rough shape dated 340 BC. Price is little tough this time, will you consult with some expert or simply buy it after negotiation on less price? In my opinion you should call police straight. Why? ; How a coin has a date on it 340 BC. Who could know that Christ will for sure be born 340 years after today and make a coin in advance at that time? Where is your focus? If you not have focus or dig down the facts you may burst into flames on your mistake, which could give you loss in terms of anything imaginable. Those who are professionals on making illusions can divert your attention, engage your mind into multiple directions, make you lose your focus and they can make you fool. What magicians do? Simple; make you lose your focus. Magicians are smart, they know at what mille second divert your attention and create illusion, which resulting that you clap for them at the end, especially kids who have immature brains. Kids always by nature have fewer tendencies to focus.

Not every stated, broadcasted statement or product especially in world of marketing and cyber media is universally suitable for every single individual from different backgrounds, lifestyle, education, profession and age group. We must seek the truth by narrowing down our focus, make rational judgement that it meeting your requirements perfectly.

It is also very important to figure out how each individual interpret it and absorb it. Let's for example take people in mix of males' females, young to old around a dozen. Make a row; turn all of them in one direction. Last person in the row will knock the shoulder take his or her attention by turning towards your face, and say few words in the ear or demonstrate certain signaling by act of hands and arms. Rests of ten people in row are not aware of what is going on at the back. When each act or whisper is passed on to next till last one, it is completely changed to almost feel like a joke. Why it happens? This behavior is lack of focusing and lack of seeking the truth and basically how we interpret it. Both interlink to each other; focus vs interpretation. Once I did tunnel farming; off season vegetable farming in controlled temperatures. By looking at the production data of previous years it was very tempting for me. I invested money and time. When time came to harvest and selling in the open market I was surprised to see how many other factors involved in determining a final price from picking to packing, carriage, toll taxes, market commissions / whole seller margins to retailers carriage, toll taxes, storage all has cost loading / offloading and eventually his margin, after all these factors price is determined. Reason I did not seek the truth. Each step involved was taking out my margin. One question arises from here; that who was responsible to check before investment. 100 % my responsibility, we will discuss in coming chapter. Directly working on self-assumptions harms and gives loss without seeking the truth. Our focus should have been like "Blondin" explained below; walking on the tightrope over the "Niagara Falls" that even on his 2<sup>nd</sup> time walking on rope successfully lifted his most hated manager over his shoulders and crossed it. Imagine his level of focus that over his shoulders the man he disliked most and each step on tightrope at fearing height over fast moving waters below was incredible. On each work if we keep our focus like "Blondin" we never fail;

Jean-François Gravelet nicknamed Blondin adopted his father's nickname born in 1824 for his fair hair stunned the world on June 30<sup>th</sup> 1859 by first tightrope-walk across Niagara Falls, Blondin offered to carry a volunteer over his back but, unsurprisingly no one stood forward. What a narrowing down his level of focus was. Richard Cavendish Published in History Today Volume 59 Issue 6 June 2009.

Blondin's first crossing of the Niagara Falls was in 1859, that was the most famous feat in a life packed with them and like all the others was painstakingly prepared, organized and exploited for maximum publicity. He took care to enlist the support of the Niagara Falls Gazette, which at first thought it was a hoax and then decided he was mad, but went along anyway. Newspapers all over the country were soon interested. The rival Niagara Mail was sarcastic in its coverage and the New York Times said Blondin was a fool who ought to be arrested, but posters and handbills boosted the excitement and were not aware of his level of commitment and focus. The railway companies laid on special trains and thousands of spectators assembled to watch. The tightrope was taken across the river in a rowing boat. More than three inches (7.5cm) thick, it sagged by some 60 feet (18m) in the middle, so it had a steep slope. The distance was a little over 1,000 feet (305m). Bands on both banks played as he began his crossing at 5.15pm and took his time over what he privately considered was an easy task. He stopped and lay down for a rest at one point and stood on one leg for a while. The crossing took him a little over 17 minutes. After a pause he went back across on the rope, much faster this time. He was cheered to the echo and the feat was reported all over America and in Europe.

In several later crossings Blondin introduced variations;
- He carried his top-hatted manager across on his back
- Crossed blindfolded
- On stilts
- In a gorilla costume and
- Pushing a wheelbarrow.

One of the wonders of the age, he built himself Niagara House in the London suburb of Ealing in 1889 and died there of diabetes in 1897, days before his 73rd birthday. He buried in Kensal Green Cemetery. Neighboring streets in Ealing, Blondin Avenue and Niagara Avenue, preserve his memory and there's a Blondin Street in Bow. His focus has been extraordinary that he crossed blindfolded; amazing act. We need such focus when going through any of the process in our life, each time we work on any subject matter.

Once narrow down your focus, truth comes out automatically. Focus brings clarity same as Hubble Space telescope does. Hubble space telescope was launched in year 1990. It is not the first but biggest into low earth orbit operational ever since, it is one of the largest and most versatile and is well known as both a vital research tool and a public relations boon for astronomy. The HST is named after astronomer Edwin Hubble and is one of NASA's Great

Observatories, along with the Compton Gamma Ray Observatory, the Chandra X-ray Observatory, and the Spitzer Space Telescope {1}. Why billions dollar product is made and launched, it has its operational cost too, It had two main objectives; a: discover big galaxies and then b: further narrowing down its focus to examine single selected star, its size, color, behavior, characteristics and distance. Since Hubble is working we are seeing wonders in the sky. It is all became possible by narrowing down focus. Hubble features a 2.4-meter (7.9 feet) mirror, and its four main instruments observe in the ultraviolet, visible, and near infrared regions of the electromagnetic spectrum.

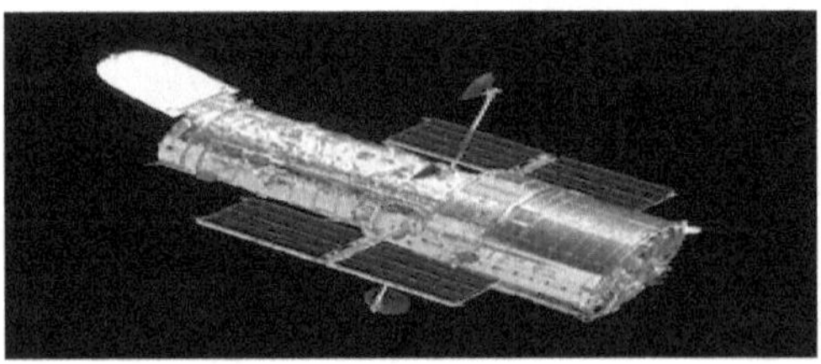

The Hubble Space Telescope in orbit as seen from the departing Space Shuttle *Atlantis*, flying Servicing Mission 4 (STS-125), the fifth and final Hubble mission. Wikipedia.

Same in our daily life, we must focus our brain to that selected single choice one at a time, object, idea, product, task same as Hubble Telescope does and create characteristics of Hubble scope in you, taste; if it is an eatable, touch feel it, hear about it from different sources, use even 6th sense; power to feel without using 5 factors, it works very well in solving problems, sit at calm peaceful place, focus on the matter. Make an analysis of the selected choice by following chart;

Effect of having it               1, 2, 3, 4, 5

Effect of not having it           1, 2, 3, 4, 5

Do comparison. If benefits of having it are 4 points and not having it loss is 1 point, meaning 3 points benefit. It helps in generating the value of your choice, important to weight points accordingly.

All most all organizations in the world people work, people come from different backgrounds, all organizations have competition with other similar organizations and within each organization again competition to take lead to get promotions, even white collar workforce while communicate, it has this feeling that sharing 100% information will enable others to take lead and get promoted so they try to share less knowledge with similar or low rank staff, even twisting the information so that no one get clarity, also their way of expressions vary person to person. Organizations also try to take lead in the market by using different techniques. Media war, marketing, advertisings etc So it is very important to seek the truth, not believe as it is conveyed to you for successful growth, do some research on your own by narrowing down your focus to that particular choice, this is the world of knowledge and competition, we all struggle to survive and to take lead. So absorbing information as it is, passed on to you by others is not rational, work on it like Hubble scope does. All organizational have cultures, without organizational culture no organization exist, so you need to study it by narrowing down your focus and by seeking the truth to survive and grow accordingly.

Especially stock exchanges affected by rumors and are very fragile to any negative incidents, news, and propaganda. So stock exchange investors should must dig down to facts and seek the truth, because speculations attract reckless investors who do not unfold facts. Stock exchanges are very sensitive to speculations but results to be expected by the intelligent investor.

There is intelligent speculation as there is intelligent investing. Speculation in not illegal or immoral, some speculation is necessary and beneficial on two levels.
1st, without speculation, un-tested new companies like amazon.com would never be able to raise capital.
2nd, risk is exchanged every time a stock is bought or sold.

 Speculation may be un-intelligent in many ways like;
A; speculation when you think you are investing rightly.
B; when you lack proper knowledge and skill for it.
C; risking more money, in speculation, than you can afford, to lose. Speculation is always fascinating, and it can be a lot of fun while you are ahead of the game. If you want to try your luck at it, put aside a portion the smaller the better, of your capital in a separate fund for this purpose.
Never add more money to this account just because the market has gone up and profits are rolling in.

That's the time to think of taking money out of your speculative fund.

Never mingle your speculative & investment operations in the same account, nor in any part of your thinking {2}.

I once attended seminar of "Darren Winter" an investment consultant of "London Stock Exchange" trading during my studies in London year 1999. I learned the best technique which applies on different areas of investment one or the other way same principles apply. Darren Winter explains;

- Look for a growing industry for example; Telecom, Cement, Textile etc.

- Check last 10 years balance sheets, check assets vs liabilities. Find stable companies.

- Pick 3 who got the most cash flow in hand. If there is cash there is dividend, no cash no dividend. Simple.

- Out of 3 see who has lowest price share and highest yield. This is the only technical part here, why lowest price like 10 USD why not 100 USD? Suppose you have 1000 USD to invest. 1000/10=100 shares. 1000/100=10 shares. Suppose yield is 5. 100 shares x yields 5= 500 or 10 shares x yields 5= 50. See the difference of lowest price and highest yield calculation and its potential output.

- Invest or buy when low in price sell when price is high. Keep in mind targeted price to sell it not too high, once achieved don't wait, sell it.


- Repeat.


What we all did above is from broad spectrum of industry to stable company and lucrative shares analysis is in fact we narrowed down the focus and digger out the truth. It is among few workable options we are looking for a choice that is best result oriented according to our objectives. We had choices all around us to buy any of the shares of any industry but finally concluded intelligent investment by narrowing down the focus and seek the truth.

Apple Company had the more cash flow as compare to US government. According to the statement from the U.S. Treasury, the government had an operating cash balance of $73.8 billion. That's a lot of money, Tech juggernaut Apple had a whopping $76.2 billion in cash and marketable securities at the end of June, according to its last earnings report. Unlike the U.S. government, which is scrambling to avoid defaulting on its debt, Apple takes in more money than it spends, July 2011, {3}.

Steve Jobs in the two years after his return in 1997, he took the company from 350 products to 10 only which means he said big NO to 340 products, that not counting anything else that proposed during that period. At the 1997 MacWorld developer's conference, he explained. When you think about focusing, you think, "well focusing is saying yes", "no focusing is about saying no", Steve Jobs was after extraordinary results and he knew that there was only one way to get there {4}. Steve Jobs was a well-focused man.

First ever ski decent July 2018 of K2 a Pakistani Peak by Andrzej Bargiel in 7 hours, total ascent time 3.5 days total decent from the height of 8611 meters through E route or point out of 6 routes mentioned earlier ABRUZZI SPUR at 8000 meter- CESEN / BASKOW ROUTE – MESSNER VARIANT at around 7000 meter – KUKUCZKA PIOTROWSKI ROUTE in middle of 6700 meter to 5900 meter till 5000 meter heights straight nose down to Base camp, it is a breath taking video can be seen on YouTube. It was a vertical drop of 3600 meter.

The world's first ski descent of K2
By Rory Smith, CNN
Updated 1539 GMT (2339 HKT) July 24, 2018. {5}

Andrzej Bargiel has become the first person to ski down from the summit of K2 which stands at 8,611 m (28,251 ft) [16].

THE K2 TEAM WAS:

Andrzej Bargiel
Bartek Bargiel
Janusz Gotab
Piotr Pawlus
Marek Ogien

Imagine the level of focus he had, one wrong step and deviation from pre-planned route or mixing of c with f route could have taken his life and,  could have taken him to fall hundreds of meters where no chance of survival, extreme cold and low oxygen. Compared to the more than 4,000 people that have summited Everest, the world's tallest mountain at 8,848 m (29,029 ft), Less than 350 people have stood on K2's peak so far which costs around $ 50,000/- USD for a person to just attempt since it was first topped out in 1954.

There are so many incidents of death every day while taking selfi. Many young guys lose focus eventually lose their life. On 24th May 2019 [Jang Newspaper] reported an American mountaineer Donald Lynn age 55 reached on top of The Mount Everest successfully, during the process of making selfi he fell from 29000 feet height, two assistants who were locals searched him, during rescue and shifting, he lost his life at point Hilary Steep. What an un-bearable loss, that few seconds loss of focus did not let him celebrate his achievement of reaching highest mountain in the world in Nepal. So, keeping your focus at the right time for the right situation is so essential in our daily routine life that we can not only succeed in life but we can stay healthy, happy longer and successful. We cannot physically present in one location and virtually present at other location, physically and mentally has to be at same point. Our brain does not support such difference as explained earlier.

My Swedish telecom equipment maker company Ericsson announced on June 2009 that Hans Vestberg currently CFO chief financial officer and Executive Vice President; who The 44-year-old Vestberg has been with Ericsson since graduating from Uppsala University in 1991, he held a number of international management positions, including serving as the CFO of Ericsson in Brazil between 1998 and 2000, and in North American from 2000 to 2002 {6}, taken over as CEO of the company in 2010. He had a proven excellent understanding of Ericsson's business with experience from all different Ericsson business activities. He has been instrumental in developing Ericsson's industry, leading services operation which grew threefold with good profitability during his five years of management.

His one of the achievement brought him to this position was, that during the world economic recession in year 2008/2009 Ericsson predicted short fall in sales / orders booking going to reduce for next financial year by almost 30 %. He was financial head of Ericsson before becoming CEO. I remember we were called for a quarterly all staff meeting and our country president Mr. Zibber briefed us on this issue. Hans Vestberg when briefed to Swedish board members in Ericsson head quarter, he just not given the bad news of less dividend to shareholders for upcoming financial years, he provided the solution too, which was approved in the board meeting and spread to all 180 countries to follow instructions, so that shareholders do not get affected by the worldwide economic recession.

Mr. Zibber briefed us that from today we need to cut cost without affecting the work, how it was possible to cut cost without affecting the work. It was possible and we did it by switching off un-necessary lights, I remember two tube lights were taken away from my room; I still had enough light to work. Imagine how much electricity cost saved if Ericsson exists in 180 countries around the world, how many offices and how many rooms in a building. The effect was unbelievable. 2ndly cut to air travel, multimedia's were installed in all offices to communicate directly as video conferences instead of travelling internationally and locally city to city, Directors given-up business class seats and travelled in economy class, only for matters of high importance were allowed to travel. I remember Mr. Zibber called next all staff quarterly meeting and we were stunt to see figures globally that approximately entire target was achieved by next quarter with few more measures taken.

What an exercise was done in a corporate sector which was the vision of "Hans Vestberg". What "Hans Vestberg" just did? An analysis of very few choices Ericsson had, from couple of choices he picked this way to reduce cost by narrowing down the focus to adopt a soft change in the way of working without affecting quality of work and job releases. We all have choices; need to elaborate by narrowing down our focuses. Like Hans Vestberg did, shareholders happy staff happy too, because no job losses.

Always do focus like microscope / Hubble power to find out either Amoeba cell or Bacteria cell, so that right medicine be prescribed or focus like Blondin; who walked on rope blindfolded and next time man on his shoulder. We can never fail. Our success chances will be maximized by just implementing on this factor only among others mentioned in this book.



## LOOK FOR 80/20 EFFECT

After you narrow down your focus, look for Effort vs Reward ratio. What is 80/20 Effect? It is the comparison of how much we can apply effort or should be to get reward for the selected choice? Ideal scenario is 20 % effort 80 % reward.

Why Question; why we have to take this choice. Why question is very important, 80/20 principle give answer. Without understanding why question or without applying it, chances are we fell into trap, trap that drag us attract us towards certain choice due to many internal factors or external factors, personal likeness, external attraction created by others. Even you narrow it down to seek the truth or taken expert opinion, still do not invest or take a start until you do 80/20 effect analysis. Once you pass this test go ahead. Choice should drop here if effort according to your personal scenario and personal capacity vs reward is not worthy. This is the point if further investment is carried on without knowing of how much effort you can place in will go into loss or without knowledge of how much effort is required and how much comfort to sacrifice to get that reward, chances are you will quit in the middle of your efforts. Why mostly people quit tasks immediately or after some time working on it? Because they don't do analysis of how much effort required to complete this job or how much comfort has to sacrifice by examining its own personal circumstances.

This theory & pattern was first of all discovered in 1897 by Italian Economist Vilfredo Pareto (1848 – 1923), his discovery has since been called many names including the Pareto Principle, the Pareto law, the 80/20 rule, the principle of least effort {1}. Pareto discovered by following the economy of nineteenth century in England. He found that most income and wealth went into hands of minority of people (20%), he also found out that there is consistent mathematical relationship between the proportion of people and the amount of income or wealth enjoyed in a group, in simple words he found out that 20 % of people enjoy 80 % of income or wealth. Then you can reliably predict that next 10 % would have say 65 % of the wealth and 5 % would have 50 % {2}. In achieving success up to here is the analysis stage from first step of picking up one small smart choice to narrowing down the focus to 80/20 effect are three steps, we must do these three-step analyses before start of spending time money health into a project, relation, best choice we selected.

We should be fast in day to day matters to do this analysis on quick basis and should not ignore by looking at the scale of matter suppose very small. Matters of large scale and high importance, make detail analysis of 80/20 effect. Next three chapters are Execution stages to reach final destiny of success. So it is important to do analysis in detail from all different aspects because after this stage there is no point of return without paying price, if we return we have to pay price like Amazon owner paid the price at the time of divorce and made her ex-wife among top richest woman in the world with billions dollars explained in earlier chapter. For his ex-wife's point of view it looks like good 20% effort and 80% reward; on a lighter note but practically it is 100% fact.

80/20 effect describes that a Minority of causes, Inputs or efforts usually lead to Majority of the Results, Outputs or Rewards. Practically & literally this means that for example 80 % of what we achieve in our job comes from 20 % of time spent {2}, we normally don't expect this, we may believe that 15 % reward required like 100 % effort or input. According to "Vilfredo Pareto" 20% right effort can produce 80% results. This is why it is so important to pick one small smart choice so that we achieve our aim more easily.

The essence of 80/20 analysis and thinking are interlinked with picking up small smart choice and gives us a practical approach that will help all of us to understand and improve life.

That inbuilt imbalance between causes and results input and outputs effort and rewards proofs of potential that majority of people have little impact and small minority have major impact and it always has potential in all fields of life. Potential word is used to give a feeling of how far an individual can get achievement for future users of this principle but in fact it has proved that 20 % of people hold 80 % of world money and resources.

Our aim should be to look for those choices where input or effort is minimum aimed at producing the results; out puts or rewards to maximum capacity or make such processes or line up activities in such way that minimum effort required producing maximum results.

This principle has very large scope and applicable on all parts of life. Think of any area in your mind where this principle does not apply, I can assure you will find none. I share couple of areas where we cannot think of that this principle cannot apply;

Now a days we live in era of life 3.0 a technological advances time period and most of us use Google Map live streaming to check traffic jams, slow traffic. This data can be observed easily on Google Map. You will be surprised to know that not all roads or junctions in a city can block or choke at the same time, its only 20 % of the places are where city traffic in charge need to work out better plans build infrastructure deploy more traffic wardens or take such measures that people commute smoothly. By self-checking of traffic jam areas before starting a journey can give you a better plan to avoid such routes, save fuel, save time and most importantly stress free drive. Working on these points can also cut down pollution these vehicles generate every second causing raising temperatures of big cities and causing severe health problems for those living in vicinity.

This principle is unique in its nature that enables us to solve problems too. Using this principle makes us enable in finding these solution easily too. Life should be easy, making complex solution is not a good sign, always make easy soft simple solutions. This is the essence of this principle. It gives us this indication that less effort more reward. So go for easy simple soft choices in life otherwise there will be more effort less rewards, unless you have self-esteem objectives in life; people who take challenge to climb up to K2 is not an easy choice, it is life consuming activity that one out of four do not climb on top. What they get out of such expensive sport that one attempt cost almost 50,000 USD per person and 75% chance of going up at 8000 meter where very low oxygen. For such people reward is not 25 % or less as compare to more effort, for them it is vice versa, there reward is not even coming in calculations.

Mother Teresa; for her reward meanings were different. She felt pleasure satisfaction in helping others. So it is important to keep difference of rewards. Her life was not easy; she faced lots of challenges, her level of efforts vs rewards were of different level and different meanings but principle 80/20 is applied in its true sense.

80/20 principle acts like a surveillance system too, if we keep it on, it can help us spot dangers and works well. Dangers exist all around us; dangers always hunt for its prey. Dangers exist in all shapes and in different types. We must not come into its way. Even make some forecasts too like we get severe weather warnings. We have dangers in business, relationships, being robbed, and adventurous sports and even we travel, we are surrounded by dangers. Our surveillance system should be on to protect ourselves. In business we have competitors, their marketing strategy or similar product can eat our product's profit, counter strategy of adding more value, lowering price and aggressive sales and marketing need to consider as per your own product or nature of danger & circumstances we discuss below;

Recently there were crashes of Boeing 737 Max 8 eventually grounded, deaths 189 on Lion Air Flight 610 on October 29, 2018 {3}, 157 on Ethiopian Airlines Flight 302 on March 10, 2019 {4}, total 346. Sensors were installed to surveillance danger; a detailed timeline suggests the pilots were struggling to deal with an automated safety system - known as the Maneuvering Characteristics Augmentation System (MCAS). A stall can happen when the plane flies at too steep an angle. This can reduce the lift generated by the wings, potentially making the plane drop.

To recover from a stall, a pilot would normally push the plane's nose down.

In the 737 Max, MCAS does this automatically, moving the aircraft back to a "normal" flight position.

The system then repeats the process if it detects the plane is still tilted at too great an angle.

However, after the Lion Air crash, it was found the aircraft had experienced problems with a sensor which calculates the angle of flight, or "angle of attack"{5}.

Why the above MCAS system did not work? It was not looked through 80/20 point of view; its failures or its malfunctioning was not taken into account that how big a loss could happen and what other benefits are associated with this system. Simplicity is the best solution, simple easy handling cause less complexities. Simplicity; easy to handle and recover. This situation can be explained like; according to 80/20 principles we should develop such systems which are simple and have alternative recovery methods instantly in case of danger, danger has to be tested in a flight simulators covering all risks, new additions must be mentioned in hand book / Pilot user manuals. Pilots were un-able to handle situation. Sensors were given wrong data, switching off MACS system by pilot and manually handling the situation was not saving the plane because MACS system was switching on again after some time, again given wrong data coming from sensors made situation verse.

Less effort more comfort, less effort more reward, less effort more simplicity, less effort more safety, less complexity more reliability, less complexity high Trust, less complexity add more value into system are areas to look into and are lessons to learn here.

Surveillance system helps us spot opportunities too. Free markets work automatically; shift resources where productivity is low and move into areas of higher productivity, let's suppose a factory is producing five different types of products, sales data shows three out of five products are top revenue generating items and remaining two are low margin producing products. Resources consumed by low margin producing two products will be 40% as compare to 60% of resources consumed by three products which are highly revenue generating products. Our approach should be to take out 40% of resources and spend on high revenue generating three items to produce more, it will bring cost down and ultimately more margins. Outsource those two low revenue producing products or sell its production or even quit manufacturing those like Steve said no to Apple 340 products and put all resources on 10 products only, it is not rational to spend 40% of your resources where there is no productivity or very low productivity, this is the main philosophy of 80/20 principle, less effort more rewards. In addition to cost there is always hidden costs and risks associated with each producing item, we can eliminate risk too by outsource or selling of manufacturing of two low revenue generating products. Eventually we moved to 100% revenue generating products and 100% resources allocated to three products will give equation of less effort = more reward; 20% effort = 80% reward. This principle is all about moving resources from low value to high value uses. Non-productive to productive manners, low margins to high margins.

There is always a waste of resources in Government sectors and big corporate sectors, there systems are over complex, bureaucratic approach and level of hierarchy slows down the process to such level that those industries associated or dependents on this system start getting affected. This is common situation and reason of non-developed countries. Such sectors carry 80% of resources and only produce or add 20% of value into the system even less than 10%, in certain situation even start eating 100% of resources and produce 0 or Nil revenue, some sectors even run on loss eat resources from other sectors, Governments keep on filling them by taking resources from other profitable institutions and burn into Nil value generating sectors. Eventually under developed countries start taking Loans from private banks then later from IMF, World Bank and start paying heavy interests. Public has to pay price of their own corrupt politicians, this loan taken can also be spent on high value generating projects if 80/20 principle is kept in mind. Loan taken can be utilized efficiently. Public sector is always slow due to its over complexity, lack of improvement mission and lack of work under 80/20 principle. If a rule is made for every individual working; to add more value and report weekly or monthly as compare to resources are being consumed and bench mark is given of 80/20 principle to produce 80% value / output vs 20% input of resources or time, sudden change will produce from individual level to aggregate level, resulting high value addition in these sectors, turning them into profitable, value added institutions. Governments should also work like free markets do; move to vital few, privatize maximum, reduce burdens, except few areas of Education Health Law & Order Etc. even these three sectors and also other nonprofit organizations can set parameters in terms of resources vs facilities, resources vs quality, resources vs value adding equation of 80/20 principle and turn into more helping hands for society, improve life standards, which is an ultimate goal of all governments.

At personal level, look for useless habits which do not give you positive rewards, eliminate those habits which occupy your time and generate less reward. Add those habits which can give you more reward plus pleasures. Work on weekly basis, find one such habit, work on it entire week. Get used to it without it and add new one. Next week find next one and add one more. You will feel the difference in a month.

Social issues analysis also resolved by this 80/20 principle. We need to figure out of what topics discussion gives us more laughter, provide happy moments, environment that gives us more peace and health and our activities that provide more satisfaction. We need to draw a table and give them numbering from 1 to 10. List down activities start giving them marks, try to start from daily waking up to bed time, write down all daily routine, free time also, eating habits too. Keep writing till 7 days that no activity is missed out; 7 days will cover of maximum areas, no chance to miss out any activity because some time we don't repeat an activity every day and do it once a week. We will have data that give sum at the end, we can find out those activities which provide maximum satisfaction, happiness; in the table below we have some activities associated with score more than six;

E = 6, D = 7, K = 7, A = 8, J = 8, H = 9, C = 10.  TOTAL = 55        +- 81%

 Same time we have marks less than five, which are;

I = 0, F = 1, G = 3, B = 4, L = 5.  Total = 13      +- 19%

We have data almost close to 80/20 means out of total we have healthy 81% happy moments which is pretty good and only 19% un-happy moments. There can be situation where 19% happy moments and 81% un-happy moments; there we need to shift drastically our habits from 19% to more and take it up to 80% at least and drastic reduction in 81% activities and bring it down to 20% un-happy or even close to zero un-happy moments. Means; simply spend more times in those activates in which you feel happy the most. Add more choices in your life in which you are comfortable. Get rid of certain low productive events.

| Serial # | Activity | 1 | 2 | 3 | 4 | 5 | 6 | 7 | 8 | 9 | 10 | TOTAL |
|---|---|---|---|---|---|---|---|---|---|---|---|---|
| | | | | | | SATISFACTION LEVEL | | | | | | |
| 1 | A | | | | | | | | 8 | | | 8 |
| 2 | B | | | | 4 | | | | | | | 4 |
| 3 | C | | | | | | | | | | 10 | 10 |
| 4 | D | | | | | | | 7 | | | | 7 |
| 5 | E | | | | | | 6 | | | | | 6 |
| 6 | F | 1 | | | | | | | | | | 1 |
| 7 | G | | | 3 | | | | | | | | 3 |
| 8 | H | | | | | | | | | 9 | | 9 |
| 9 | I | | | | | | | | | | | 0 |
| 10 | J | | | | | | | | 8 | | | 8 |
| 11 | K | | | | | | | 7 | | | | 7 |
| 12 | L | | | | | 5 | | | | | | 5 |

This type of exercise applicable to all areas of life, we can use it to multiple production units, draw a table giving most generating revenues and profits to least lucrative products, take data from sales department, apply same concept. Give more attention to the most profit giving products, shift maximum resources, increase production, lower down the cost etc.

Some relations are by default when we are born, some relations we make in our life through our choices, friends are totally made through our choices in life. 80/20 principle help identify good relations and friends too. Make a list of 1 to 12 relatives and friends; give them marks 1 to 10 same as above in the table. Data will provide you top quality relations and friends you feel happy among them, spend more time with those you get more pleasure and avoid those who are least supportive, least innovative, least energetic, least knowledgeable, least productive, least caring, least full of laughter, least positive, least achievers in life. Human is a social animal, social circle very important to live healthy life. Since I know this rule, I moved more into reading books, more into climbing mountains on safe tracks because I am not professional mountaineer, I standing on top of the mountain absorb fresh breath, views most beautiful nature. Play more squash, at least an hour, sit with friends in beautiful park discussing all sorts of topics from new inventions to present political scenarios, sports etc. I feel fresh throughout the day, I eat more healthy foods, drink more water and I love the life.

The true joy in life comes from spending time with people who constantly inspire nourish and replenish your soul.

This 80/20 practice make you get free time, work less, earn more, enjoy more. We need to make our habit of thinking 80/20, it is light thinking and do not require huge effort but impact is so powerful.

Articulate your life through this philosophy; express your thoughts more frequently and positively more clearly with precision. You can get rid of thoughts which convert into your language of ill nature. Become an 80/20 thinker it generate more actions and make sharp improvement in life. This improvement will attract others and they will love to be in your company and you can convert yourself in the list of others at top scoring marks about you, similarly the way you feel happy about some of your top marked friends, relatives they will feel about you the same way. We must move our time energy money same way like industry move from less productive to more productive items, ultimately we will have less effort more rewarding life, less problematic more happy life, I observed we don't do simple things, 80/20 is simple way of shredding negativity adding more positivity.

Find out most happy moments with those who satisfy your inner soul, be among those who are sincere, knowledgeable, pleasant, achievers, skip rest slowly who depress you and not having eagerness to move forward for better life for themselves and for others. When I go out tracking mountains or hunting with friends I count effort vs rewards, tracking on mountains is a tough job sweating, thirst, hunger, tiredness but I find reward is 99% when reach top, witness breath taking views of nature which we do not see in daily life and feel my effort was just 1%. I feel my life has extended to a year due to fresh air pumped into lungs, heart beat works opening of arteries veins, more oxygen to brain, and muscles get maximum work out. What else we need!!! Remember always; be top achiever in all areas of life, small small achievements add up and work like a compound effect will be explained in coming topic.

"Learn how to separate the majors and the minors. A lot of people don't do well simply because they major in minor things ".                                                  - Jim Rohn- {6}

We need to shift from minor good to major Good. This is the essence of 80/20 principle.

Almost all of the businesses have clients, they buy our products, generate revenue for us.  Sometime we give goods & services on credit for short term or medium long terms. We must have dates when they pay us back. Missing commitment of dates will also be available, we can make table like above used to identify who are the top ranked fulfilling commitments and who are not. Give more importance and value to those who are high scorer.

Staff performance and their outputs can also be measured and reflect their score in the table used earlier. It is easy to get rid of low performers 20% staff and invest to those who give 80% output so that they deliver 100% performance. There are thousands of examples that employee get homes cars lucrative share in business because they deliver 100% to company. World's Top No. 1 restaurant for many years "noma" in Copenhagen Denmark I visited once; on reception I found out a month advance booking required, I was stunt. "noma"; given its staff members, shares even to (chef) in company ownership. He must have been high performer. Business owners must make top performers part of their team so that their system become 100 % efficient. It adds more value to the systems resulted more reward to the organization. Surprisingly "noma" is a simple restaurant from outside as seen in below picture, my visit in 2012.

Optimism & Enthusiasm are not only enough to be top achiever; it will not work to succeed unless smart choice selected, narrowed your focus, looked for 80/20 effect, be proactive, lined up activities and worked as compound effect. Optimism & Enthusiasm will work only if prior detailed working is completed which are six steps in this book, then Optimism & Enthusiasm will work and give result. Most of the people work on jobs they don't enjoy, here Optimism & Enthusiasm that good job will come one day on their way, will not work. Working required in getting a dream job. Optimism & Enthusiasm is a trap for those who think that by showing it things happens automatically; it's not. Those who just wait do not plan carefully, select choice carefully, and focus carefully it will not work for them.

We cannot change the world if we do not believe that progress is must responsibility on every single individual on this planet in every field of life. We cannot improve relations if we don't believe in progress. We work for getting better positive results which is called progress. Negative results means, lack of working and focus, selecting a wrong choice. Purpose of life is to avoid negative results. Only 20% of right resources really matter in terms of top achievements, it means humans are capable of immense and uncountable abilities and only require 20% right working to outclass others according to Vilfredo Pareto those 20% who possess 80% world's wealth has done the same, it's amazing. Therefore give attention to right 20% factors and resources to get 80% results and rewards. Saying no to unproductive resources is very important otherwise we can't improve our self our life our business our job our friends our time etc. some people have problem saying no, they think it's rude or un-polite but you need to change this habit. As I mentioned earlier; Steve Job said big NO to 340 of its product lines and made Apple the most profitable company in the world. So make courage and power to say no to non-productive areas.

Sacrifices vs Rewards; when kids are born, mother sacrifices her sleep and has to work hard in taking care of fragile new born, but reward she gets is best in the world when toddler looks into eyes of his / her mother and smiles.

In this world nothing is free; every single factor has its cost. This cost is in terms of many shapes; time, physical effort, sacrifice to comfort, mostly has to spend money to get it, health and sometime relations. In ancient times when soldiers were going to fight wars, what they had in their mind reward means that their next of kin, family friends and entire tribe will live in peace and safe. Many sacrificed their lives, lost arms legs etc. why? Reward for them is too high, living for others. Many young people move to other cities for better education & jobs, they sacrifice their comfort of home and relations.

You are better judge of your own situation and circumstances, what effort you can make and for that outcome, once you do your initial homework then go for expert opinion. Never work against laws of nature and do not apply effort vs reward principle where; honesty, respect, kindness are compromised, no matter how big reward is, it will be temporarily and unjust, you may kill right of others to get reward. What these drug dealers do? They kill humanity. World is changing very rapidly but these fundamentals will never change. Animals do not have moralities, they live on the principle of "Survival of the Fittest", while during my university study period in London, I heard many incidents of foxes invading houses through windows and picking and killing month old babies. Animals are cruel; we must not act like them to get rewards. Helping others; do not look it through effort vs rewards. Helping others; reward cannot be calculated in terms of monetary benefits, it is beyond human capability to think of what is the reward? Rewards of helping others come from un-known directions and at un-known timings, which may not be immediate. People who ease the life of others or end their sufferings are the dearest to God.

It is a decision making point either to go ahead with selected choice or drop it based upon 80/20 effect through study and focus on subject matter (choice). It is entirely your decision, even it can suite you 40 efforts 60 rewards or 50/50, effort vs reward. It may suit you even 70 efforts 30 rewards, according to your situation but potential exists 20 effort 80 rewards.

Remember! You can quit in middle if not measured in advance of how much effort you can put in place. Once mind is clear with calculations, just go ahead for the selected best choice.

# BE PROACTIVE 100% YOUR RESPONSIBILITY

Who will do work on your Goals, Missions & Objectives? It is only you 100% responsible. It is only you who can make yourself successful, no one else.

This is the first practical step, Take Initiative; waiting for something will happen is not the right approach neither it will work. Now for every single activity you need to take a start, follow it through, till completion you are 100% responsible and no others, even you have people working for you. Even if you have partners still you responsible in case anything goes wrong, selection of right partners who are 100% responsible too is your 100% responsibility. Hiring of 100% responsible staff is also your 100% responsibility.

"A sign of wisdom & maturity is when you come to terms with the realization that your decisions cause your rewards and consequences. You are responsible for your life and ultimate success depends on the choices you make".

-Denis Waitley-

Robert W Mitchell, The Awakning Word: Being called to the spiritual path. (Author; House, 2011) p. 62.

Before early steps given in this book were examining the subject matter; either yes or no. if yes is the signal; it is time to act now.

Suppose you are starting a construction unit. After all the analysis you concluded that construction industry is booming and is a lucrative business. In fact you are selecting one project at a time and it is small smart best choice, you narrowed down your focus and seeks the truth that among all industries construction industry is more lucrative business at the moment. And housing need has instant demand in market. Then First step you will have is to look for appropriate capital to complete and deliver the project on time with profit after all taxes paid. You came up with a unit cost of each apartment and compared with market price. You consider it safe investment; effort is 40 rewards are 60, after all the working and you are happy about it, instead of 20 effort 80 reward. For some people 50 effort 50 reward will be enough. Suppose you have 70% capital, next step is to visit at least two banks for financing the project because you do not have 100% capital. You need to get up and walk towards bank. One Bank with best services and low rates signs a deal with idea of early booking through bank sales team and a special counter in bank branch for sales to secure clients; Fantastic. Next step is to look for real estate experts at least two to look for an ideal plot location. It is 100% your responsibility to buy well in budget and at top location, easy approach, with surrounding facilities. After buying property, you are 100% responsible to hire at least two architects. One's Plan is ideal, drawings are ready. Now it is your 100% responsibility to get it approved from building authority a local government body. Now it is your 100% responsibility to hire marketing companies at least two. You sign a contract with one of them which is having vast network and different media channels like; paper, online, TV commercials, personal networking etc. next step is 100% your responsibility to plan a sale price and launch an early booking through bank with announcing a ground breaking ceremony. Marketing company; covering events, launching aggressive sales marketing plans. It is your 100 % responsibility to hire a management consultant who is having proactive attitude and construction experience, who will plan and track down every single activity. It is your 100% responsibility to create a purchase department, which consist of honest and proactive people who get you material in budget limits, not compromising quality and on time in case you are to arrange material of your choice and design. You have five stakeholders or companies working for you at the moment, a bank, an architect, marketing company, it is your team, and you are 100% responsible in arranging them. In case of any mistake you are not to blame one of them it is you who need to make sure checks and balances are created, experts are hired, on time or early errors are detected and rectified, later it will cost you more and you will run out of finance and time. Virtual models are run, it help detecting errors in advance.  Clients are booking apartments. After completion it comes the hand over stage on time is nailed your success and your 100 % responsibility paid off. Your teams are supporting your goal but it's only you 100 % responsible. In case of delay or failure, who will be sued or taken into court of law? It is you not the bank or marketing company or architect, so ultimately all the activities are dependent on your working on time and right steps taken. If you think you just made a plan and people will do it automatically. It's like you are a very nice and vegetarian person facing a lion in front of you and thinking lion will not eat you because you will not harm or kill him, reality is not like this, lion will kill you and eat you. Projects and world is same like lion. World will eat you if you are not protecting yourself, in this case your finance or project, and it is only you who is 100 % responsible in protecting it and deliver it on time. Previous three steps are not closed, they go along till completion or till delivery of project, keep looking 80/20 effects philosophy in every single activity, train people to always look through this approach and every transaction should be filtered by 80/20 effect, always keep narrow your focus seek the truth, always go for smart small choice one at a time, it is a constant practice.

What is the act of entrepreneur? [In this situation are you] "Pro Active", you did all things, you initiated all things, and you were not sitting back and waiting for things to happen automatically. To be Top Achiever; you have to be Pro Active. Proactive approach is one of the key among other keys. Without proper working like selecting one small smart choice and then narrowing down focus to seek the truth and then further do 80/20 analysis, Just being Proactive will not work, more likely chances of error, because working on base with knowledge is very important and previous three keys steps help avoiding mistakes.

Healthy people are Pro Active People who intake right food right fluid & enough sleep of at least 8 hours in dark room even no tik tik of clock sound;

"According to the new research less sleep from 8 hours can aged a person decade more than actual who take proper 8 hours sleep, sleeping before and after learning is as important to save learning in memory same way we hit save button on computer, 40% less memory brain ability discovered in MRI data of a group out two; one did not sleep for 8 hours as compare to full 8 hours sleep group, found healthy signs of learning found who had full 8 hours of sleep, by putting electro on head discovered very powerful brain wave happened during the deep sleep called sleep spindles act like file transfers from short term vulnerable portion of reservoir to long term permanent part of brain and making them safe, 1 hour of sleep deprivation on clock change in winter and summer found sleep loss and its effect on cardio vascular; 24% more heart attacks are discovered very next day due to 1 hour of short sleep hours among global experiment performed on 1.6 billion people across 70 countries twice a year called day light saving time, in winter 24% reduction in heart attacks, same effect in car crashes and even suicide rates, natural killer cells in immune system suffer just from one night 4 hours of sleep caused 70% reduction, short sleep is short life, two groups of healthy adults were taken and one group restricted to 6 hours for a week as compare to other group of 8 hours of sleep caused DNA distorted of genes by 711 other half increased by 50% which had full 8 hours sleep".

[Matt Walker; Brain Scientist TED April 2019. Sleep is your Superpower]

Imagine that how much our brain and body being affected on less sleep is explained above that we cannot stay Pro Active on this evidence, so sleep well.

Fewer intakes of nutrient or junk food and less fluid cause low energy level. Low energy level cause laziness. Lazy people sit back and wait for things to happen, lazy people slow in thinking slow in moving slow in decision making on time, they may take decision when right time has passed or arrive at train station when train has left the station. Low energy leads to low self-esteem; low self-esteem means less interest in surrounding, lack of motivation, lack of competition, lack of positivity, lack of willingness to improve in any field of life, I have seen two of my hostel mates coming back from airport who missed their international flights on different dates. What a laziness can be; un-imaginable? It is not only laziness; they were reactive people instead of Pro Active people.

Reactive is the opposite of Pro Active. Reactive people, who wait for things to get over, then stand up and look around what was that when it is over. Slow in finding, slow in observing, slow in figuring out; what is the share of his or her in it, late in deciding, late in figuring out opportunity from any situation. Reactive people mostly complainant. They always have reason to complain and they stick to it. Never learn from mistakes. Never be reactive, be Pro Active. Also those who don't take enough on time sleep mostly fall into this category as well. What a waste of life!!!

Balance nutrient diet, reasonable exercise convert to a balance energetic body, which is very important to perform active routine life. There are lot of charts of balance diet online and books available. Reasonable exercise chart according to age are also available. I will not go into this detail. Essence is; to do any sort of activity we all need proper intake of food and liquid daily. I have seen many people coming late in office and saying not feeling well, on asking mostly, reason is late sleep etc. and mostly delay matters to later stage to complete, this bad habit makes lot of work parked un-attendant ultimately create mess, create panic for themselves and most likely incomplete work with error.

History of shops are not very long, before shops people use to trade as exchange of goods called barter system, before that we were all hunters, we have to hunt to survive. No hunt no food, no food then starvation and ultimately death. Because no shops, people were very Pro Active because lazy person cannot do hunt. In a second prey can disappear. Accuracy also comes if we are Pro Active. Hunt is a skill. Prey never comes straight and fell in front of us to hunt, lot of precise focus, energy, accuracy, timing and running required to hunt down. Before humans had not enough tools to hunt, now a day we have telescope, guns, sound that attract birds or animals, data available with wild life, permits are issued for certain locations where population is more than required. In many countries like Canada, freezer limit also allowed of certain birds in a permit. Before no hunter had such facilities, he or she has to be very Pro Active to hunt down bird or animal. They had to walk or run after many miles and target from a certain distance. Before the invention of fire there were no tools. Fire made us able to make swords, knifes, arrows etc. before humans have to hunt down with sharp stones. What a tough life our ancestors had in the biological life 1.0. We reached today's comfortable life by selecting smart choices & by focusing.

Earlier human's main objective was to survive from many dangers like; tough weathers, dangerous animals, self-cure from diseases because no doctors available just practice of elders was the only method to cure from disease, knowledge was passed through generations. People had to act fast, not sit back and relax. Today's available facilities on door instantly made us lazy. We can order pizza, deliver to us in twenty minutes. What effort is required, just a phone call.

Why we make a loss? We may have right choice, right capital, high scoring academic staff but not Pro Active team. People working in stock exchanges are very Pro Active. They keep track of data, world affairs, politics, and new technologies all the time, take decision immediately when they think is appropriate to either buy or sell stocks. If they sit back and relax their game is over.

Pilots flying planes especially fighter jets are very Pro Active people, fraction of a second miscalculation and lose of focus can break apart millions dollars machine in seconds due to its high speed.

Success Nailers are very Pro-Active people and 100 % responsible to every single activity, even they have people working for them, those people are also hired by them who ultimately run the show. So, you are 100% responsible of outcomes, because you hired them.

Pro Active is a takeoff point. It is a key to perform and complete on time activities.

Postponement & Procrastinator is a disease and illness. Many people have this habit to postpone any type of work including breakfast lunch and dinner which should be on time to be active healthy life. If we not healthy we cannot perform well. When we keep postponing work, it aggregates and then no chance left to focus on which one to complete first. This is the stage of panic now and cannot complete all works at the same time, impossible. Remember I explained in start one small work at one time to keep focus is important, multitasking is not supported by our brain, chances of errors will be high. Never ever let this situation arise that you are surrounded by activates to complete and you are running short of time. it is a habit that can affect your health too. If you are facing bruised eyes, dizzy feelings, do not feel eating etc. and not getting your Doctor appointment, problem may get complicated and you reach at last stage to cure well, what is the benefit of postponing work which need your attention right away. Right away it can be fixed easily on low cost, later high cost high risk.

Biggest rewards are found out of comfort zone.

All the inventions are not happened automatically, someone tried to do something, either research & development in large organizations or self-experiments by individuals. This is all due to Pro Activism. Discovery of atom, Creation of Bulb for light, discovery of germs, reaching up to moon and then mars all this became possible due to Pro Active habit and effort to move forward and do not sit back and relax.

In football who keeps ball in possession or makes a goal? The one who is Pro Active; the one who runs after ball, beat opponent by running faster than opponent, carry and kick ball in opponent net. Have you ever seen among 22 players football in the possession that is not running and standing still and making a goal?  You will never find such player and will never see any goal. Goal is possible through legs of Pro Active players only.

Pro Active is a person who makes things to happen and done on time, he or she makes things completed accurate on time instead of waiting for them to happen automatically.

Those who nail into their success are not super intelligent people or very high graders; instead are Pro Active, 100% responsible people and honest, rest them learn very quickly. Pro Active people eager to move forward and do not sit back and wait for things to come to them, they reach out to understand, learn and adopt. They will best listen and act on time and proved to be helping hands for you. They take 100% responsibility whatever task given to them to complete.

When you are Pro Active & 100% responsible, look for Pro Active & 100% responsible staff, further train them how to look for small smart choices one at a time and keep your focus to seek the truth then adopt philosophy of 80/20 principle or effect anything they do, you will have best team working for you, then if you are not there watching them, what and how they do, they will come out with best results automatically. Let them do, initially they may lack few things because they are learning quickly, you need to supervise and provide guidelines initially, do not get worry if few mistakes are made, mistakes will be truly upgrading them. Repeating same mistake is bad; monitor those as given data in below table. Keep this chart on your table, keep looking and adding score in chart,

| | | | | | | | | | |
|---|---|---|---|---|---|---|---|---|---|
| | | **Staff Performance 80/20 Table** | | | | | | | |
| Staff | Honest | Pick Small smart choice | Narrow Focus Seek Truth | 80/20 Thinker | 100% Responsible | New Errors | Repeat Errors | Job Skill | Total Score % Age |
| A | 10 | 8 | 8 | 8 | 9 | 2 | 10 | 9 | 80 |
| B | 8 | 6 | 6 | 6 | 8 | 1 | 6 | 7 | 60 |
| C | 8 | 6 | 6 | 6 | 8 | 1 | 6 | 7 | 60 |
| D | 10 | 8 | 8 | 8 | 8 | 12 | 10 | 8 | 80 |
| E | 8 | 6 | 6 | 6 | 7 | 1 | 5 | 7 | 60 |
| F | 5 | 5 | 5 | 5 | 5 | 5 | 5 | 5 | 50 |
| G | 5 | 5 | 5 | 5 | 5 | 5 | 5 | 5 | 50 |
| H | 10 | 8 | 8 | 8 | 8 | 2 | 10 | 8 | 80 |

Less Error More Points

in a month you will have people who are high performers medium performers low performers and you will have results in terms of 80/20 principle, you will have data that can give you information that A, D & H are those on them you will have 20 effort and 80 output, B, C, & E are those on them you will have 40 effort and 60 output, rest F & G 50 effort and 50 reward.

Repeat this cycle again, similar people can be hired again and divided into two groups simultaneously as per your situation. If you think you can improve 40/60 group retain them, work on them. Move them into 80/20 category, not all people have same brain, same backgrounds, same brought up, but you have one system running, bring them on board as per your requirement. Align them according to your system in place. For me one of the great & best thing you can do to someone is; upgrade his / her life, let them stand on their legs with your support, ultimately they will support you in doing right work for you. They will earn to run their family, kitchen. Further grow and flourish their life with your little help, ultimately a happy society emerge from dark. Reward you get is not the only work you get in return; it is un-imaginable! beyond any calculation, and this reward you get not from that person but from elsewhere, a Haven.

Jack Ma; Alibaba.com founder world top few richest people in the world, As of June 2019, he is one of China's richest men, with a net worth of $35.6 billion, as well as one of the wealthiest people in the world and also was ranked 21st in Forbes' World's Most Powerful People {1}, Who is top visionary who changed the world from traditional shopping to online shopping; e-commerce.

He was rejected from job interviews 30 times; for Police job 5 people applied for job 4 accepted and he was the only rejected, KFC; when it came to china first time, he said 24 people applied for the job, 23 accepted, he was the only rejected, went with cousin for hotel job again rejected. He told himself in front of his mother luck has not arrived yet but actually he was persistent and proactive keep on looking for his job, one day he will has his day, something somewhere waiting for him but not today, constantly perusing. He applied 10 times to Harvard University, 10 times rejected. Now he can teach Harvard. He says learn from your mistakes, mistakes are great mentor. Jack Ma is the great inspiration for the many young professionals now and gives speeches to world renowned platforms like; world economic forum, time magazine, American Express forum, South Africa investment summit, SABC News talk, Tel Aviv University, UN Chief Digital Cooperation talks etc. he has been awarded so many titles not because he postponed work, instead eager to grow, Pro Active and responsible 100% whatever is delegated to him or assigned to him, most importantly; whatever target he set for himself, he manages 700 million users on alibaba.com. He encouraged his 70 founders that if we successful 80% of young people can be successful. This is the responsibility he transformed among his companions.

REWARDS / HONORS OF BEING PRO ACTIVE
&
100% RESPONSIBLE

In 2004, Ma was honored as one of the "Top 10 Economic Personalities of the Year" by China Central Television (CCTV).

In Sep 2005, the World Economic Forum selected Ma as a "Young Global Leader".
Fortune also selected him as one of the "25 Most Powerful Businessperson in Asia" in 2005.
Business week also selected him as a "Businessperson of the Year" in 2007.
In 2008, Barron's featured him as one of the 30 "World's Best CEOs"
In May 2009, Time magazine listed Ma as one of the world's 100 most powerful people. In reporting Ma's accomplishments, Adi Ignatius, former Time senior editor and editor-in-chief of the Harvard Business Review, noted that "the Chinese Internet entrepreneur is soft-spoken and elf-like — and he speaks really good English" and remarked that "Taobao.com, Mr. Ma's consumer-auction website, conquered eBay in China. He was also included in this list in 2014.
BusinessWeek chose him as one of China's Most Powerful People.
Forbes China also selected him as one of the Top 10 Most Respected Entrepreneurs in China by in 2009. Ma received the 2009 CCTV Economic Person of the Year: Business Leaders of the Decade Award.
In 2010, Ma was selected by Forbes Asia as one of Asia's Heroes of Philanthropy for his contribution to disaster relief and poverty.
In 2011 it was announced that one of his companies had gained control of Alipay, formerly a subsidiary of Alibaba Group, so as to "comply with Chinese law governing payment companies in order to secure a license to continue operating Alipay.
Numerous analysts reported that Ma sold Alipay to himself below market value without notifying the board of Alibaba Group or the other major owners Yahoo and Softbank, while Ma stated that Alibaba Group's board of directors were aware of the transaction. The ownership dispute was resolved by Alibaba Group, Yahoo! and Softbank in July 2011.
Ma was awarded an honorary doctoral degree by the Hong Kong University of Science and Technology in November 2013.
Ma is a board member of Japan's SoftBank and China's Huayi Brothers Media Corporation. He became a trustee of The Nature Conservancy's China program in 2009 and joined its global board of directors in April 2010.
In 2013, he became chairman of the board for The Nature Conservancy's China Program; this was one day after he stepped down from Alibaba as company CEO.
In 2014, he was ranked as the 30th most powerful person in the world in an annual ranking published by Forbes.
In 2015, Asian Award honoured him with the Entrepreneur of the Year award.
In 2017, Fortune ranked Ma second on its World's 50 Greatest Leaders list.
In 2017, a KPMG survey ranked Ma third in global tech innovation visionary survey.
In October 2017, Ma was given an honorary degree of Doctor of Science in Technopreneurship from De La Salle University Manila, Philippines.
In May 2018, Ma was given an honorary degree of Doctor of Social Sciences honoris causa in recognition of his contributions to technology, society and the world by University of Hong Kong.
In May 2018, Ma received an honorable doctoral degree from professors Yaakov Frenkel and Yaron Oz at the Tel Aviv University in Tel Aviv, Israel.[19]
In May 2019, Ma and other 16 influential global figures were appointed by UN Secretary-General Guterres as the new advocates for sustainable development goals.

He quit teaching after six years in school, in 1994 when most of us knew nothing about what computer is, and what is going to be internet, what will be the use of internet, Jack Ma invited his 24 friends and briefed for two hours, 23 said forget about it, one said try it, if did not work come back. They said it will not work, because there is no such common thing internet in the world, no credit card online payment methods, especially you know nothing about computers. Jack Ma said after whole night thinking in the morning I decided I still want to do it, because most of us have fantasy thinking during the night and next morning they do still the same job and forget about night dreams. He was the one who went against 23 of his friends. China was not connected vastly via internet in 1994 but during his visit to US, he experienced about internet. No mobile phone in china. In 1999 he made alibaba.com. He invited his 18 pupils, briefed them for two hours again, briefed them future of internet. He believed in future this internet will work and China will have future in the e-commerce. China internet speed so slow still no mobile phones, no logistics, no payment methods, but Jack Ma believed e-commerce will have its future and will change China. He continued to work hard and believed his company will be among top 10 in the world, they gathered money but was too difficult. His dream was to help small business through e-commerce. In America that time e-commerce was to save cost of big companies, Jack Ma went opposite by narrowing down its focus and seek the truth, helped small business to reach out market via internet as we call it online now a days, Jack Ma approach was right to facilitate small business which has the most versatile products made with care and passion that do not have sources or money to reach out local and international markets. He believed small business know how to make money we just need to facilitate them is the small smart choice.  He helped them to promote on the internet. He found no payment mechanism, he said let's build payment mechanism [Pro Active Approach], he found no logistics, he said let's build logistics mechanism [Pro Active Approach], after almost two decades he is over the top in e-commerce because he calculated effort vs reward 80/20 principle. He says never give up if you have a dream. Lot of people talk dreams but do not convert into reality, who converts them into reality? Proactive & 100% responsible. Make your dreams realistic, and make them happen.

He further believed and aimed that alibaba.com will be the 5th largest Economic entity around the world beside; US, China, Europe, Japan.

What a Pro Active approach is and making himself 100% responsible to achieve it. He believed when you have two to three million dollars it is your money, when you have around 20 million dollars you go into better stocks options due to devaluation, and when you have around 100 million that money is not yours, it is social responsibility that people trusting you, ask you to manage money better. He aimed for economy big enough that every young man or woman and small business enables global buy global sell global delivery global pay and global travel with technology, we are providing goods globally from single website because it has less efforts more rewards, we can create 100 million jobs for the world, today we create 33 million jobs for china and we can enable 2 billion people shop anywhere and can create 10 million small business who can profit. This is his vision given by him to Tel Aviv university students.

So far he has shipped around the world $ 550 billion dollars till year [2016] from the day they started worth of goods and bigger than 21 countries GDP, Bigger than Argentina economy. His website delivers 65 million packages in a day; amazing he started from self-purchase of 21 items because nobody was buying it speaking to Nairobi University 2017.

Due to technological world is moving very fast, we don't know what world & data will look like in next thirty years. But we are sure world will change in next thirty years. Innovation has released physical power of humans and machines have taken over, as we see excavation, loaders, dumpers, tanks and cargo planes etc. in next thirty years technology will liberate brains, machines will function automatically, think on their own, not controlled by human brain. Machines will communicate to each other, analyses and will take decisions own their own.

Next business models will be business to consumer (one to one) because we have lot of data available of consumers from different sources like; Facebook or other apps and manufacturer will customize products for them accordingly and specifically. Machines will just not make products; machines will think and talk. Machines will not be linked with oils; machines will be supported by data and electricity. Business will not focus on standardization; they will focus on flexibility, customization, quickness and user friendly.

Future is not muscle power; it's the wisdom, care and responsibility. In next thirty years how clicks and motors work together is not digital economy, in fact a data economy. It's not the technology that changes the world, it's the dream behind the technology ream that changes the world, and it's the Proactive vision that changes the world. Before 1903 man had a dream to fly; now aviation is a whole big industry. Jack Ma had the dream to introduce small business to Europe through internet before 1999, now alibaba.com linked globally. His dream built infrastructure online and now among top few companies in the world sending products to your door step globally called e-commerce. He had dream when no mobile phones in China, no logistics, no payment methods even very slow internet. He nailed / resolved it through being proactive & being 100% responsible.

100% responsibility means responsible of delivering success and delivering results. Suppose when coaches are hired to make a team for Olympics or world events, they are appointed to win. They are 100% responsible to deliver victory. The entire exercise from start of announcing the tournament date till final match 100% responsible to develop training program designed to identify first each players Mental /Social/ Physical / Game level then analyzed training requirements of each individual players accordingly, not one training for all; It will help to drill down weak areas of individual, so this customized training program will bring up excellence. Last but not the least with one clear aim to bring championship title in home they needs to work together as one team by Placing in Planned Long Term

Variation and progressive overload of training called "lining up activities" in all respective fields of game.

First of all it is 100% responsibility to hire a right person, who further takes 100% responsibility to deliver results, and he / she must cover every aspect of related fields like briefed above. Corporate level projects demand exactly the same treatment. Successful delivery of projects is exactly the same like bringing championship trophy home. Same detailed working required covering all aspects and lining up activities smartly to nail your success.

King of Squash; Jahangir Khan, a legend who won 555 international matches in a row marked his name in Guinness book of world record. Five years unbeatable. No super athlete can beat his 555 continuous matches win record from this planet for the hardest game in the world "Squash".

Notable achievements
- Won World Amateur Championships at age 15.
- Youngest ever World Open Champion at age 17.
- Unbeaten in 555 consecutive matches over 5 years and 8 months.
- Won the British Open Championship 10 times in succession (1982–1991).
- Six-time World Open Champion.
- First player to win World Open Championships without dropping a game.
- Played the second longest match in the squash history 2.46 hours.

The Mighty King of Squash, The Conqueror: JAHANGIR KHAN

In 1979, the Pakistan selectors decided not to select Jahangir to play in the world championships in Australia, judging him too weak from a recent illness {2}. Jahangir decided instead to enter the World Amateur Individual Championship and, at the age of 15, he became the youngest-ever winner of that event. Pro Active and taken 100% responsibility to produce result even though not recovered fully from illness.

The Government of Pakistan honored Jahangir with the awards of "Pride of Performance" and civil award of "Hilal-e-Imtiaz" (Crescent of Distinction) for his achievements in squash. They also awarded him the title of Sportsman of the Millennium. 

How he achieved this? For his training, he would often start his day with a 9-mile (14 km) jog which he would complete in 60–120 minutes at a moderate pace, followed by short bursts of timed sprints. Later he would weight train in the gym finally cooling down in the pools. He would follow this routine 5 days a week. On the 6th day he would match practice and rest on the 7th day. Wikipedia.com

He also said that he has experienced running on every surface: from custom-built tracks to asphalt roads, grass & farm fields to sea shores & knee-deep waters. Sometimes he would also visit the northern areas of Pakistan to train at high altitude in low oxygen conditions, a great proactive approach.

In 1990, Jahangir was elected Chairman of the Professional Squash Association, and in 1997, Vice-President of the Pakistan Squash Federation. He was elected as Vice-President of the World Squash Federation in November 1998, and in October 2002 was elected WSF President. In 2004, he was again unanimously re-elected as President of the World Squash Federation at the International Federation's 33rd Annual General Meeting in Casa Noyale, Mauritius. Wikipedia.com

Time Magazine has named Jahangir as one of Asia's Heroes in the last 60 years. Jahangir Khan was conferred with an honorary "Doctorate of Philosophy" by "London Metropolitan University" for his contributions to the sport.

Due to his immense and absolute dominance in squash he was nicknamed "The Conqueror" {3}

He has been the most Pro Active athlete in the world. This much success cannot come as luck. There is an immense working behind it. God helps those who help themselves, no one will come and give you something in your hand, in case of world championship, opponents will not let you win and let you hold trophy unless you work for it, it is you and only you have to be Pro Active & 100% responsible.

In terms of making good relations; I missed many good people in my life because I was not Pro Active & shy  in taking initiative to say; "Hello How Are You", later I did not get chance to see them again.

Use any source of motivation triggering +vie waves for you like, good weather, upcoming events, use of profit on dream vacations etc. When you are Pro Active, you do things on time and are punctual with appropriate actions. Time is asset, yesterday cannot be recovered, today is quickly disappearing, and tomorrow is waiting for us, if we not ready and utilized time well it will become another wasted day, so be a good user of present time and well prepared for tomorrow, why not start right away and keep going to "nail your success".

# LINE UP ACTIVITIES & REMOVE DISTRACTIONS

Since the evolution of business & corporate world it is so much written on management sciences, high level of degrees and even Doctorate Degrees are in process around the world in top Universities. I am talking about overall management concept relates to all fields of life and not just limited to business management. I my-self "Master of Business Administration" specialized in "Strategic Information System Planning & Designing" from UK and almost ten years of Ericsson working experience; a world's top Telecom company, I believe end of the day management science is simply; "lining up of activities in relevant boxes, in relevant perspectives, defined sequences to be performed on right time with appropriate cost effective resources efficiently, keeping in mind quality is the essence regardless of activities belong to any sector of life".

All successful people simply line up activities, place it smartly and then work on it one by one.

Mount Everest or K2 climbers line up activities of every day tracking schedule, make and prepare their bags accordingly, collect stuff needed as per their lined up activities like tents, ropes, stove, minus 30 to 50 degree centigrade sleeping bags, torches, emergency satellite phones, diet plans etc.

Simply think of activities related to anything you are going to do, write activities down and make a list of it. Key rule is do not miss out any smallest activity even very tiny nature of it, some-time very small activity of less importance block remaining part of the process or remaining activities to be completed. Suppose on K2 summit expedition you have missed cliff hanging clips, you can-not take even single step without it. Cost of cancelling the expedition is too high, cost of delaying the expedition very high too at this point.

In complex projects it is called project management, in complex projects but in simple terms called line up activities, and according to the activities prepare an item lists needed. Why we missed clips, we had not enough focus and got distracted at the time when list of activities is being made or lining up of activities.

So, success nailers keep their focus like Blondin, who walked on tightrope over Niagara Falls, and kept removing distractions, while walking. Blondin has been keeping control by judging wind pressure & rope vibrations, ignoring sounds, ignoring visuals, except looking at his rope and feet.

More organized projects or people tag items with activities and make dependency charts. Dependency charts and flow charts help resolve issues. Advance stages projects, people make charts and run visual programs. Visual programs help resolve almost entire issues.

Coke has developed such unique recipe with certain lining up of activities / materials, certain quantities, and certain sequences that many tried to copy and develop same taste but failed, Coca Cola the iconic beverage has kept world's most highly regarded trade secret 125 years of special moments and history the legendary secret formula in "Coca Cola Vault museum Georgia US" where no human allowed to go.

Before going into tunnel farming project, I should have been running a visual set up of taking crop from my near-by farms and sell it into the market without investing huge infrastructure of control temperature tunnels, then grow vegetables harvest it and then selling to open market. On selling I came to know that many factors were affecting the price, which I was not aware of mentioned earlier. So do small part by part visuals, if possible run entire practical visual. Large organizations make demos run virtual programs. Make a habit of doing so on your even small works. Now a day's virtual reality can take you on top of mountain Everest while sitting in your room, you feel like walking among other mountaineers or even walking on the moon. Detailed human body organs are best explained and give exact feeling how they work in virtual reality; you can even be inside blood vessels and travel with red blood cell to any part of body.

To live as successful people, we need to adopt the strategy from very early age by teaching our kids to start lining up activities in a manner that we all live as successful people live, repeat below again:

Small smart choice one at a time like Ericsson grew till 5G
Narrow down your focus like Blondin & seek the Truth
Seek 80/20 effect of less effort more rewards
Be Pro Active & only you 100% Responsible
Line up activities smartly & remove distractions
Compound effect Consistent & Accelerate


We need to drive our self towards what successful peopled do, simply line up activities for our self and arrange lining up activities for your team; working for you, makes it easy for them to work and perform. Rests they will do well and deliver own their own because your team consists of proactive people.

Once you start lining up activities for yourself and for your team, your set destiny or targeted outcome start appearing and start visualizing, this small success one after another builds confidence and helps in completion & in overall success.

With the help of virtual model all activities lined up & flow chart built by my-self of a complete process of work in setting up new Base Transceiver Systems in September 2004 and started operation, with set days to be completed a single activity time line and resources involved helped me delivering project before deadline, I beat management expectations which helped soft launch in January 2005 a turn-key project (from zero to on air live calls GSM) covering & connecting 28 big cities and commercial launch on 23 March 2005. We were testing call qualities in January 2005. I got performance award on multi millions dollars Telecom Network Deployment & Integration Project from Ericsson in acknowledgement of launching a telecom company in 28 big cities in shortest period of time, acknowledge by Warid Telecom CTO (chief technical officer) Mr. Marwan at international forum.

Just to give demonstrations of how games are built, activities lined up in below given flow chart marking sequence, task, and dependency resources involved;

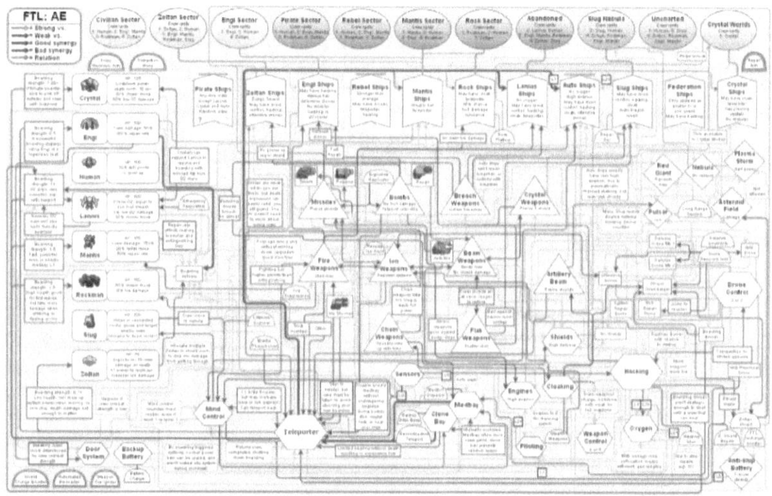

Game Software lined up activities with sequence

In simple situations, simply list down step by step activities involved from start till end. Write them even minor or smaller impact has in the process. Keep the same sequence as it is required to complete the task, review it again and again so that no single activity is ignored.

Let's work on resources required in hunting, based upon lining up activities we required following resources or goods to complete the expedition. Any skip of single item may ruin entire trip, so very important to list down entire process one by one. Mostly for hunt we travel that far end where no shops nearby available where we can buy relevant item. Cross checking from other experts can add professional opinion but still 100 % responsibilities lies on your shoulders to provide and pack every single Item in the list. Same way projects are planned, materials, resources, time is calculated. Below is the list prepared for tracking expedition as a template, each plan may vary its list based upon geographic location, number of people and type of track. Basics are simple list down activity planed step by step and relevant items required:

| | Items | Quantity |
|---|---|---|
| Drinks | water | 1.5 ltr x 40 |
| | water purification drops | 1 ltr |
| | cofee ready mix packs | .5 Gram x 40 |
| Cooking | cook stove & pot | 2 |
| | stove fuel | 40 ltr Gas |
| | cofee cup, spoons, plates | 5 each |
| | camp water reservoir | 1 |
| Toiletries | toothbrush paste | 5, 2 |
| | wipes | 15 packs |
| | moleskin for blisters, rope, | 1 sheet |
| | tylenol, Ibuprofen, allergy meds | 1 pack each |
| Food | garonal bars 4 for each day / person | 60 |
| | hot oatmeal | 15 |
| | trail mix | 1 |
| | crackers 6 packs for each | 30 |
| | ckicken broth 6 each day | 18 |
| | herbs dry, spices | 18 packs |
| | gum | 18 sticks |
| Clothing | hat, merino wool base layer, socks, trousers, golves | |
| | rain jacket, down vests, jacket, blankets, | |
| Equipment | rangefinder, bow & accessories, bear spray, watch | |
| | bugle, binoculars, sunglasses, backpack, straps, shelter, | |
| | sleeping bag, led tent light, torch, alarm, gps, headlamp, | |
| | extra battries AAA, wind checker, face paint, licences, permits | |
| | pen, camera, knife, map, orange flagging ribbon, lighter, duct tape, | |
| | super glue, garbage bags, hooks, rope, hammer small, belts, | |

While lining up activities be flexible, rigid plans hard to change and costs more on revision, even slight change if required.

There are two approaches to work on a process;

A: simply go by the sequence as required regardless of small or big, most important or less important.

B: Do strategically most important activity first then 2$^{nd}$ and then on and on but problem with option B is difficult to calculate comparison, which activity is more important to others and is time consuming.

Listen to others too, pay attention, absorb value adding advice only, rest ignore. Biggest chains in the world achieve mastery of lining up activities then supply chain is improved to keep rhythm and momentum with similarity in products and services. Before achieving mastery their lined up activities are flexible to change till perfection is achieved then no change to keep symmetry in products and services e.g' McDonald burger taste & look the same all over the world.

Once, activities are lined up then start execution one step at one time or one activity at one time, or assign one activity to one individual and 2$^{nd}$ after 1$^{st}$ completion then on and on. Standard times should be calculated for batch productions, it is easy to checkout performance of individual resources and this way easy to find out performance by applying 80/20 formula.

Break large activities into small steps until single activity is lined up and fully visible and un-folded. Entire scope has to be unfolded into single activities, mark numbering and give sequence as given above in game software. It is called WBS "work break down structure" according to PMI Global

Standards Project Management Institute; Page 49 PMBOK 4<sup>th</sup> Edition Project Management Book of Knowledge.

Further PMBOK describe it in more academic terms;

Define activities; is the process of identifying the specific actions to be performed to produce deliverable.

Sequence activities; is the process of identifying relationships among the deliverables.

Estimate activity resources; is the process of identifying the type and quantities of material, people, equipment or supplies required to perform each activity.

Estimate activity durations; is the process of approximating the number of work periods needed to complete individual activities with estimated resources.

Large projects further connect activities like flow charts or develop virtual models to identity exact costs, quality, risks involved and how to mitigate. Looking for alternatives reduce cost, reduce risks. Keep on sticking with one idea not recommended, it can delay damage and increase cost. Always look for alternatives & make a habit of keep looking for alternatives. It applied to all areas of life.

As long as we are alive, we get distracted all the time from events happening around us all over the world or some with so close and with immediate effect that cause distractions like road accidents happen every day due to on live call while road crossings. Anything we do, or in any thing we are involved, we get distracted from other people's point of view, impactful visuals and most importantly when we are dependent on others. In real corporate world when processes are being developed or activities are being lined up, special focus is placed to remove distractions. Removing of distractions makes job easy for all stake holders performing the tasks. Environment is created in such a manner that people stay on focusing their activities till the time they complete their job. Operation theaters are designed to stay focus on patient surgery, direct heavy spot lights overhead, tools lined up, relevant staff surrounded, and machines tested working perfectly, then step by step procedure or operation. No one allowed knocking doors and entrance closed. Precision, timing and completion of lined up activities required one by one. Distraction is matter of life and death.

Most of the road accidents and collisions are due to physically present at one point and mentally or virtually present somewhere else, taking phone calls are banned due to this reason of distraction that cause fatal accidents.

Animals also get distracted and being hunt especially in traditional hunting methods, hunters use to make traps to distract birds and animals. Fishing with rod is one of the simplest examples that fish only focus on fly attached with hook and do not look or care about hook and gets hunted easily. Life is the same; many of us get hooked to wrong place, wrong people, and wrong activities just because attraction is basically a distraction. International politics diplomacy unfortunately has adopted same philosophy.

Magicians mainly perform based upon distracting audiences while performing magic and create illusions. They get audience involve so much in one activity that no one aware of something else has happened at same time, which become a magic. Instead of audience should be worry of where their focus was? Start clapping; this situation is worrying point for me. In projects slight distraction cost's millions dollars.

In sport it cost's losing a match and eventually out of game or out of tournament, then wait for next coming event or next coming world cup, by that time may be your organic time to perform best is over and may be you are not in best body shape. So remove distractions in any form of life even making or living in relations, some lack of care lose a relation. One of my closet childhood friends whom I spent nearly early 20 years of life and met every single day, later I moved to another city lost him due to cancer, his brothers, doctors and he himself was distracted for many months from a chronicle disease is being spread inside his body called "cancer", eventually we lost him at his age 40 when discovered cancer has reached last stage and un-curable. His elder brother once knew about cancer, spent 2 years day and night like shadow of him, and spent hundreds of thousands of dollars to treat his cancer. He cried like hell on his distraction towards his brother that why he did not pay attention on him when cancer was at early stage and should have been investigated / cured earlier, we all cried. Doctors briefed entire family that it is not curable and let him go to The God but his brother insisted to Doctors to continue treatment, left his own family and business behind spent 24 hours with him but it was too late.

In today's fast world, there are many Time Robbers, find out who Rob your time. Time Robber also distracts you from your aims or during performing your activities. So much use of mobile is the biggest Time Robber now a days. Look around you and examine your entire day, you can find at end of the day who Robbed your time. Catch your Time Robber every day, in a week you will have sufficient time with you to utilize on many productive matters. Kids are being robbed by mobile and computer games, excessive use is bad, send them to play grounds to have physical games as maximum they can play, let them exhaust, this way you can save them from negativity. Remember physical health important to perform all sorts of tasks! Time flies very fast and no second life.

Sometime people do not get your point or do not want to agree with you not on merits just because either they are not capable or are competitors start spreading negative voices on your ideas, projects, goals, never get distracted on their voices, they may want you to be distracted from your success, it is common in real competitive world because you are going to take their market share if succeeded. Make & select your target audience carefully so that you get appreciation and solutions rather than distractions. Negative voices or people are like toxics, keep them away from you. If not, you will start struggling towards two different directions, one your actual work and second those people to whom you will start convincing and second will be your Time Robbers.

"Keep away from people who try to belittle your ambitions. Small people always do that, but the really great make you feel that you too can become great" -Mark Twain-

Mark Twain, Mark Twain at your fingertips, ed. By Caroline Thomas Hamsberger, (Cloud, Inc, Beechhurst Press, Inc, New York, 1948), p 354 & & Robert A Fiacco Author of book; Discover Your Treasure p, 89

Young kids making their career get distracted by bad company, easy money etc. it is very crucial time for the youth and for their parents not to get them distracted, it is the most immature stage, once it is passed kids and their parents will not regret entire life. This is the time to take small smart choices and success in making career.

Distractions can attack at any point, even close to winning the game and lost; once at Gouma Egypt on 22 April 2019 international match of Squash (PSA); karim Gawad 2 games up vs Omer Mosad then 3 games down. Why he lost while he was winning the match by 2 games up from best of five games? He started distracting from actual play instead looking the game as has won in 3$^{rd}$ and 4$^{th}$ game, in 5$^{th}$ game he started worrying and lost entire match. Distractions are in many shapes, celebration before actual time is distraction too. On the other side, opponent focused on better play, winning the points by playing better shots and kept the momentum going, which resulted 3 consecutive games won even though first 2 games were lost. Moral is; never lose the focus otherwise people are waiting for the opportunities to take lead over you.

Once Einstein saw the needle of the compass at the age of four, he always understood that there had to be "something behind the things, something deeply hidden" (page 46 Book The 8th Habit author Stephen R Covey) can affect or influence your activities in the middle of your success, so always look around, narrow your focus seek the truth and keep protecting your mission to succeed.

Most of the distractions occur during afternoon, two American psychologists; Mareike Wieth and Rose Zacks presented this and other insight problems to a group of people who said they did their best thinking in the morning. The researchers tested half the group between 8:30 am and 9:30 am, and the other half between 4:30 and 5:30 pm. These morning thinkers were more likely to figure out solution of the problem {1}. For most of us, mornings are when those guards are on alert, ready to repel any invaders. Such vigilance often called "inhibitory control" helps our brain to solve analytic problems by keeping out distractions {2}. And just as the studies of school performance in Denmark and Los Angeles suggest that students would fare better taking analytic subjects such as math in the morning, Wieth and Zacks say their work "suggests that schools designing their class schedules might perform best in class such as art and creative writing during their non-optimal compared to optimal time of the day" {3}

Distractions can also be at any time if we are not physically fit or not taking enough fluid and balance diet create distractions, feel dizzy, more chances of errors. Body struggles to keep up momentum and focus. I use to hate naps, I use to believe who take naps are lazy until I followed research about naps. Naps, research shows; naps improve cognitive performance and it boost mental & physical health, one well known NASA study found out that pilots who napped for up to forty minutes, subsequently showed a 34% improvement in reaction time and a twofold increase in alertness {4}. The same effect rebounds to air traffic controllers, after short naps, their alertness sharpen and their performance climbs {5}. Italian police officers who took naps immediately before their afternoon and evening shifts had 48% fewer traffic accidents than those who did not nap {6}. An afternoon nap expands the brain's capacity to learn, according to the University of California – Berkley study. Nappers easily outperformed non-nappers on their ability to retain information {7}. In another experiment, nappers were twice as likely to solve complex problems as people who did not nap or who had spent time in other activities {8}. The overall benefits of napping to our brainpower are massive, especially older we get {9}. Naps overall improve health. A large study in Greece, which followed more than 23000 people over six years found that, controlling for other risk factors as % less likely as others to die from heart disease {10}. Napping strengthens our immune system {11}. Medium to shorter the nap is greater are the effects, longer the nap is; brain starts confusing either it is nap or a sleep. An Australian study published in the journal "Sleep" found five minutes nap did little to reduce fatigue, increase vigor, or sharpen thinking. But ten minutes nap had positive effects that lasted nearly three hours. Slightly longer naps were also effective. But once the nap lasted beyond about the twenty minutes mark, our body and brain began to pay a price, that price is called "sleep inertia" {12}.

So, best thing is to re-load re-fresh feeling by taking nap. It also replace the time of low brain energy to active brain, chances of distraction reduces. Healthy brain and body make you excel and outperform in all fields of life. Struggling body and brain pull you backward. It is the time of afternoon you should take nap between ten to twenty minutes. Do not let distraction come your way, re-load or re-gain and refresh your body. Treat your body like a state of the art machine. Normal machines get heat up if twelve or more hours of continuous working are going on especially machine that has longer age. Same is the human body depends on your physical age. Use scheduled napping as a countermeasure to sleepiness and to avoid distractions and longer active working hours.

Afternoon time is the most deadly. In the United Kingdom, sleep related vehicle accidents peak twice during every twenty four hour period. First period is between 2 p.m. and 4 p.m. the other peak time is 2 a. m. and 6 a. m. same research findings of traffic accidents are in the US, Israel, Finland, France and other countries {13}. Very precise timing of un-productive hours of a specific workers found out by British Survey is 2:55 p. m. when we enter this period of time during the day; we often lose our bearings {14}. So to be vigilant this is the best time to take vigilance break or nap, to avoid distractions.

Restorative breaks increase results. Danish school children who take the tests in the afternoon score significantly worse than those who take the exams first half of the day. Researchers found this behavior other than schools too. When the Danish school students had twenty to thirty minutes break to refresh or eat, play and chat before a test, their scores did not decline, in fact they increased. A restorative break causes an improvement that is larger than the hourly deterioration {15}. That is, scores go down in afternoon but scores go up by higher rate after restorative breaks.

I wrote this book 99% in 1st half of the day and by taking restorative breaks. It helped me in being more productive and innovative each time I sit down writing.

# COMPOUND EFFECT & ACCELERATE

Keep on working with the consistency on selected small smart the best choice is a compound effect. Every second you will be distracted and your focus will be taken away by internal and especially external factors, your job is to master the art of continuous work with consistency, and do not expect results before achieving this level. Once level of mastery is achieved, results will pop up automatically like popcorn bursts; takes a leap in the air un-folded in flower shape after getting right temperature and treatment.

"Compound effect" in fact in simple terms; reading a book of two hundred pages takes eight days if twenty five pages are read daily. Nine days if one day is skipping, ten days if two days are skipping, keep reading is for eight days is compound effect. Days skipped are in fact due to distraction. To achieve goals on time, same time distractions is to be removed, it is the biggest enemy in achieving targets on time. Distractions; off track you. Reading 30 pages & sometime 35 pages is "acceleration". Acceleration play important role in meeting targets achieving goals even before time.

Initially working on your subject matter may not be efficient or accurate, but repetitive work will enable you to achieve quality, accuracy, timely. Take help if needed but don't practice wrong, this way you may become master of inaccurate ways of working. Hit that hammer where required with right force, on time. Make a habit of flawless working then keep doing. Painters have years of practice making beautiful art of hand paintings on canvas. They carefully choose colors, divide canvas into sections, draw lines and fill colors to look like a real scene in front of us. In a few days master of art level cannot be achieved, it requires years of practice. Beautiful art pieces are the result of compound effect.

Jack Ma alibaba.com founder thought of making a company in 1994 when computer appeared in the hands for business purposes. His right working continuously for five years enabled him to officially register his company in 1999, even though there was very slow internet in china, no logistics, no mobile phones & no online payments method available. On many occasions he was distracted by his friends and colleagues that you know nothing about computers but his determination, commitment and consistency for years removed all the distractions and became worth billions of dollars' company and has the potential of converting its website into 5th largest economy in the world beside 5 countries. He is standing successfully at this stage due to compound effect and by removing distractions.

Compound effect is basically productivity, practically increase and multiply productivity with the repetitive work. It is the productivity that makes us successful and top achiever. Repetitive work without productivity is like throwing arrows in the air. Arrows must be thrown towards its target and hit. Mastery is the next level of productivity; mastery is achieving extra ordinary results. Jack Ma has achieved this level in the field of e-commerce and he is the best in online trade.

Always build a chain of repetitive work with productivity is producing a mastery and do not let it break is a compound effect & acceleration in your work, ultimately "nailed your success".

Achieve small targets every day, even very small in size, will boost your confidence. Next day add more confidence and aggregate to compound effect and helps removing distractions because you will discover something is happening and adding value, making the difference. This is the productivity and achieving the mastery.

"I will persist until I succeed. Always I will take another step. If that is of no avail, I will take another and yet another. In truth one step at a time is not too difficult; I know that small steps repeated will complete any undertaking".

-Og Mandino-

If you take a look people who are really successful they are consistent / persistent & accelerators, which mean applying compound effect philosophy to their vision, you will never achieve anything big in life if you are not applying compound effect and remove distractions immediately as it appears.

King of squash and the conqueror; Jahangir Khan could not win 555 matches in a row against top players and in top championships; if he has not been consistent / persistent & accelerator.

I once was tracking in Shankargarh over the highest mountain range of Karakaram little off side from Astore to Skardu towards K2 second highest summit in the world in month of June 2019, i Spotted off track among many stones an 8 kg stone beautifully crafted by consistent & persistent flow of water 24 hours a day for years making layers on very hard stone. Instantly I shouted that's the one I am looking for and carried this 8 kg art piece made by nature and walked for 2 hours and 15 minutes, a very memorable track of my life with beautiful scenes around. When I found it, I was writing this chapter [compound effect] I decided to show the readers of this book that if hard rock can be shaped due to compound effect then why we cannot achieve what we want to be in life relates to any subject matter by being consistent and persistent we aim for, if we adopt philosophy of compound effect. I believe this stone after big bang of this universe more than thirteen and half billion years ago first time touched. It was lying among many other stones since then waiting for to be picked, it is on my side table now will rest forever. Before, time to time it has been lurking with flow of water when heavy flooding from top of hills, otherwise most of the time it was covered under snow. This summer it appeared to show the world; effect of compound efforts. It must have been lying in river or lake when water level was high; it stayed there ever since till water level went down.

Photograph Take by me

Compound effect will take us there to the point where we can celebrate success. Compound effect is the key to success among other keys like; picking up small smart choice one at a time then narrow down your focus to seek the truth then look for 80/20 effect then be Pro Active 100% responsible to deliver, further line up activities and then mighty compound effect & acceleration will give for sure guarantee a success.

Area of Shankargarh lake Dirla Bala; Photograph Take by me summer 2019

Essence is just keep on doing one right thing after another. Compound effect is like; drop of water on same spot for days will make hole in it, water is soft, rock is hard but still soft object can make hole in hard object, just because consistence & persistence, acceleration give results early and before actual delivery time.

John Calvin Coolidge was an American politician and lawyer who served as the 30th President of the United States from 1923 to 1929 gave best statement about Persistence is;

"Nothing in the world can take place of Persistence.
Talent will not; nothing is more common than unsuccessful men with Talent.
Genius will not; unrewarded genius is almost a Proverb.
Education will not; the world is full of educated people.
Persistence & Determination alone are Omnipotent".

Quoting Calvin Coolidge: 'Press ON'," Staff & Guest Blog. PBS. May 24, 2011. http://www.pbs.org/wnet/tavissmiley/blog/staff-guest-blog/quoting-valvin-coolidge-'press-on'/.] & Robert A Fiacco Author of book; Discover Your Treasure p, 96

When we apply Compound effect it means gradually increase the pace of effort, power, time, energy required. Initially effect will be little but as time goes by and mastery is achieved impact will be huge. It is same like if you drink on your way to work a cup of coffee cost you $4 per day for 5 days a week; equal to $20, you just spent $80 in four weeks, it is $1000 in a year and in 20 years it cost you $51833.79. It means any amount you spend today can benefit you around 8% in future; this is why banks give us interest rates because of inflation or devaluation of currency in future. Do you know one dollar you spend today, in twenty years cost you $5 and in thirty years $10. Let's make a habit of saving $4 a day 5 times in a week and enjoy BMW in 20 years. This is the power of compound effect; if not driving you will have $51833.79 in bank for some other purpose. Why not we save same on the day of your child born and spend it on his/her higher education at the age of 20, when this money badly needed to every young guy wishing to complete higher education. This is the power of investing on compound effect.

On the other side if we spend $100 today it is worth $492.68 in twenty years on 8% interest, here we need to make smart choice either it is worth this much amount or not spending right now, rather invest it. This way small investments time to time can make you financially stable for the later age when you cannot work that hard and with weak bones.

From the very first job at age twenty three and from the very first salary you received, can manage your own separate pension fund or provident fund if $ 250 a month is saved and invested on 8.3%. At the age of sixty-seven you will have your own $1,336,466.77 [ $ one million plus] in addition to government provident fund or gratuity.

Base Amount: $250.00 monthly investment for 45 years at Interest Rate: 8.3% (yearly). = $1,336,466.77 one million +

| Year | Year Deposits | Year Interest | Total Deposits | Total Interest | Balance |
| --- | --- | --- | --- | --- | --- |
| 1 | $3,000.00 | $153.98 | $3,250.00 | $153.98 | $3,403.98 |
| 2 | $3,000.00 | $415.76 | $6,250.00 | $569.74 | $6,819.74 |
| 3 | $3,000.00 | $699.27 | $9,250.00 | $1,269.01 | $10,519.01 |
| 4 | $3,000.00 | $1,006.30 | $12,250.00 | $2,275.31 | $14,525.31 |
| 5 | $3,000.00 | $1,338.83 | $15,250.00 | $3,614.14 | $18,864.14 |
| 6 | $3,000.00 | $1,698.95 | $18,250.00 | $5,313.08 | $23,563.08 |
| 7 | $3,000.00 | $2,088.96 | $21,250.00 | $7,402.04 | $28,652.04 |
| 8 | $3,000.00 | $2,511.34 | $24,250.00 | $9,913.37 | $34,163.37 |
| 9 | $3,000.00 | $2,968.77 | $27,250.00 | $12,882.15 | $40,132.15 |
| 10 | $3,000.00 | $3,464.18 | $30,250.00 | $16,346.33 | $46,596.33 |
| 11 | $3,000.00 | $4,000.70 | $33,250.00 | $20,347.03 | $53,597.03 |
| 12 | $3,000.00 | $4,581.76 | $36,250.00 | $24,928.79 | $61,178.79 |
| 13 | $3,000.00 | $5,211.04 | $39,250.00 | $30,139.83 | $69,389.83 |
| 14 | $3,000.00 | $5,892.55 | $42,250.00 | $36,032.39 | $78,282.39 |
| 15 | $3,000.00 | $6,630.63 | $45,250.00 | $42,663.02 | $87,913.02 |
| 16 | $3,000.00 | $7,429.97 | $48,250.00 | $50,092.98 | $98,342.98 |
| 17 | $3,000.00 | $8,295.65 | $51,250.00 | $58,388.64 | $109,638.64 |
| 18 | $3,000.00 | $9,233.18 | $54,250.00 | $67,621.82 | $121,871.82 |
| 19 | $3,000.00 | $10,248.53 | $57,250.00 | $77,870.35 | $135,120.35 |
| 20 | $3,000.00 | $11,348.15 | $60,250.00 | $89,218.51 | $149,468.51 |
| 21 | $3,000.00 | $12,539.04 | $63,250.00 | $101,757.55 | $165,007.55 |
| 22 | $3,000.00 | $13,828.78 | $66,250.00 | $115,586.33 | $181,836.33 |
| 23 | $3,000.00 | $15,225.56 | $69,250.00 | $130,811.88 | $200,061.88 |
| 24 | $3,000.00 | $16,738.27 | $72,250.00 | $147,550.15 | $219,800.15 |
| 25 | $3,000.00 | $18,376.54 | $75,250.00 | $165,926.69 | $241,176.69 |
| 26 | $3,000.00 | $20,150.78 | $78,250.00 | $186,077.46 | $264,327.46 |
| 27 | $3,000.00 | $22,072.28 | $81,250.00 | $208,149.74 | $289,399.74 |
| 28 | $3,000.00 | $24,153.27 | $84,250.00 | $232,303.01 | $316,553.01 |
| 29 | $3,000.00 | $26,406.98 | $87,250.00 | $258,709.99 | $345,959.99 |
| 30 | $3,000.00 | $28,847.74 | $90,250.00 | $287,557.73 | $377,807.73 |
| 31 | $3,000.00 | $31,491.09 | $93,250.00 | $319,048.81 | $412,298.81 |
| 32 | $3,000.00 | $34,353.83 | $96,250.00 | $353,402.64 | $449,652.64 |
| 33 | $3,000.00 | $37,454.18 | $99,250.00 | $390,856.82 | $490,106.82 |
| 34 | $3,000.00 | $40,811.86 | $102,250.00 | $431,668.68 | $533,918.68 |
| 35 | $3,000.00 | $44,448.22 | $105,250.00 | $476,116.90 | $581,366.90 |
| 36 | $3,000.00 | $48,386.40 | $108,250.00 | $524,503.29 | $632,753.29 |
| 37 | $3,000.00 | $52,651.44 | $111,250.00 | $577,154.74 | $688,404.74 |
| 38 | $3,000.00 | $57,270.48 | $114,250.00 | $634,425.22 | $748,675.22 |
| 39 | $3,000.00 | $62,272.91 | $117,250.00 | $696,698.13 | $813,948.13 |
| 40 | $3,000.00 | $67,690.52 | $120,250.00 | $764,388.65 | $884,638.65 |
| 41 | $3,000.00 | $73,557.80 | $123,250.00 | $837,946.45 | $961,196.45 |
| 42 | $3,000.00 | $79,912.06 | $126,250.00 | $917,858.52 | $1,044,108.52 |
| 43 | $3,000.00 | $86,793.72 | $129,250.00 | $1,004,652.24 | $1,133,902.24 |
| 44 | $3,000.00 | $94,246.56 | $132,250.00 | $1,098,898.80 | $1,231,148.80 |
| 45 | $3,000.00 | $102,317.97 | $135,250.00 | $1,201,216.77 | $1,336,466.77 |

"My wealth has come from a combination of living in America, some lucky genes, and compound interest."

Warren Buffett, 2010

Finance is very important factor in our lives, we must adopt the habit of saving and investing for long terms even very small amounts, we must teach our children the importance of saving and investing and rest compound effect will do the magic.

Our eating habits can also be controlled on this formula; let's work on two different angles, one; dropping of un-healthy food daily from your intake, two; add healthy food in daily intake, healthy diet charts are available according to age and life style easily online and in books.

The impact of dropping un-healthy food can be measured in terms of calories, suppose we drop 150 calories of un-healthy food daily and replacing with healthy nutrient balance diet means combination of protein, carbohydrates and reasonable good fat. Add 40 minutes' walk five days a week at least, at least two days of work out in a week with some exercises, proper sleep of at least 8 hours, early go to bed and early rise will not show you difference of improvement in first few days but after some time like couple of weeks you will find yourself Pro Active, energetic, not feeling dizzy all the time and over all your body in shape and weight loss by end of 30 days. "Health is wealth" I heard from elders since I was school going to make us eat such foods even it did not taste well. Elders taught us to perform well physically and mentally by eating proper food and not go for taste only. At that age all kids go for taste and not aware of nutrient diet plans. It is parent's responsibility to make kids aware of eating healthy food. Without eating healthy food, cannot stay Pro Active longer, soon will start deteriorating.

Keep on doing this routine will do its magic and is a compound effect. You will lose extra fat, buildup of muscles and strong bones. Ultimately you are going to have two benefits, safeguarding from disease, building healthy life style.

On the other side if we add 150 calories of junk food daily, not having any exercise, nor any good sleep sitting watching TV most of the time, in couple of days it will be hard for you to take stairs and go up to any 3$^{rd}$ or 4$^{th}$ floor. Your breath will let you feel like suffocating; very high heart beat can damage you badly. Eventually after some time some sever health problems. Then your money will be going to be wasted on medication etc. some people quit adopting good habit after few days due to slow progress initially, but only persistent people get the results, they know the effect of compound philosophy is large after some time.

"The accomplishment of any good is the progressive accumulation or compound effect of small steps taken consistently over time"

Darren Hardy author of Book; The Compound Effect

Life is all about adding one good thing after another regularly to be successful, otherwise life will go on without any achievement, animals don't achieve anything in life except effort to survive from different dangers, same situations will be ours, and we just survive and live on the edge of different risks, any time can slip and fell miserably. At later stage if survived cost of recovery is very high.

So let's overall change our attitude towards positive start; believing on compound effect, learning at least one small thing every day, drop at least one bad habit of suppose waking up late hours, let's start waking up as the sun rises, its natural way of life, birds animals wake up too this time. Many things you can do according to your situation and level of already adopted good healthy life styles. Book authors do not write books overnight, books are the result of compound effect; every day writing two pages or more persistently and consistently produce good books eventually.

We all can convert this planet into healthy free from crime if we do this practice of adding at least one good habit and leave one bad habit every day collectively. Compound effect can change our life in both ways but right positive use can only benefit us.

So compound effect is;

Turning small habits into big changes.

Small Smart Choice + Consistency + Time = Radical Difference.

Darren Hardy author of Book; The Compound Effect

You can even look smarter by adopting this philosophy and there is no limit on using it, just don't lose the grip; not losing a grip on your activity is compound effect. Losing a grip is in fact distracting from your objectives and activities you do. Pause is ok, but distraction is not good. Sometime good to take pause, it regains energy, refresh your mind for more productivity.

Patience is the key to achieve results. Sorry for those who want success in seconds minutes or hours? There is no such way; all have to be patient after applying continuous efforts, need to gear up and catch the momentum and stay in motion for achieving more and more results. Staying in motions or catching up rhythm should be tracked down which will help gradual increase in pace.

Suppose you are to run London marathon of 42.195 km. you can run 20 km maximum in one go. You need to start preparing yourself; at least a year in advance with daily increase running by 200 meters to your actual normal daily target of 20 km. In thirty days you will increase your walk to 26 km. next month 32 km, after three months 38 km, eventually after three months and twenty five days you will be able to cover 43 km distance. Now it is time to accelerate; create rhythm and catch up momentum, speed up to complete distance in shortest time period to beat world records; the 2017 London Marathon was held on 23

April 2017. It was the 37th running of the London Marathon, an annual mass-participation. Mary Keitany won the women's race, setting a new women-only world record with a time of 2:17:01 [47] while Daniel Wanjiru came first in the men's race in 2:05:48 [48]. Without acceleration and catching rhythm / momentum & acceleration it is not possible to even reach close to 2 hours 5 minutes and 48 seconds of world record. Then learn how to breathe, body posture and right stepping. Fitness with healthy diet is basic requirement to make another world record, fitness and healthy diet not only required for athletes but in all areas of life is the basic requirement to succeed, even in corporate world, projects, assignments; we always need energetic people to perform well.

If pause is required in between heavy exercise to regain energy, one day running and one day rest is good then 400 meters to add in every alternate day practice, still it takes you 3 months and 25 days to complete 43 km target if started from 20 km stamina. Acceleration is the key in progress.

Do not over do in first attempt, gradually improve, in beginning, it will be tough but when rhythm & momentum is in place, it will become an easy task and acceleration will take us there at winning point. Make a long term plan because compound effect comes after long term effort and not visible in short term.

During our work we lose our focus sometimes; because once we are awaking in the morning, we are constantly distracted due to external environment as long as we see, hear, meet people and take phone calls whole day till the time we sleep again.

The Great Greek Philosopher (384 BC - 322 BC) once said;

"Give me a child until he is 7, and I will give you a man" [49]. His meaning was getting any personality from him in return he will work through philosophy of persistency on fresh organic mind and not let him distract.

There are two main sources of input;

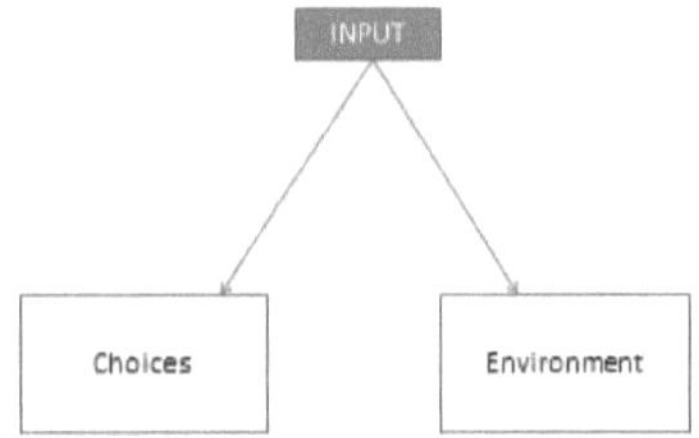


Choices are also partly influenced by external factors; difference is, choices should be from self-effort to grow better through research and development or narrow down the focus, 80/20 analysis etc. it is whatever you allow your mind to fill with or body to absorb / act is in your control, your brain is an empty box fill it with productive positive subject matters and get rid of negative effects. Stand vigilant & guarded from environment or external factors, it is our 100% responsibility to find out that; are you under any influence? for example we mostly cannot lose weight due to influence of taste of what we eat without seeking the truth of nutrient ingredients healthy or un-healthy diet but we just eat as addiction of taste. Make a habit to filter out negative effects. Make a daily routine of it.

It is in fact power to say no. Those who cannot say no; cannot achieve. To be Top Achiever you must learn and build power to say no to those distractions which can halt your consistency & persistency. Compound effect will not work if you are keeping on distracted; essence is kept on removing distractions. Power to say no can be built from right analysis, self-confidence and accurate time to say no. Those who cannot say no in fact do slavery of bad choices. Saying no is an art, sometimes say no tactfully, and sometimes delay it, sometimes partially no it according to your situation.

Use Compound effect to "nail your rock-solid success".

# SUCCESS IS NOT SIMULTANIOUS

# SUCCESS = RESULT OF RIGHT STEPS / CHOICES

Are you spending your life with this hope that few things will drop from sky one day or situations will get better soon automatically or success will drop from sky automatically? you are living in the heaven of fools and it will never happen unless you work for it.

There is no shortcut to success; success is a sequential logical move towards a big aim or purpose. Probability of a success through luck is close to zero. Suppose on the table of an American Roulette are 0 to 36 digits that becomes 37 boxes vs 1 box you picked to place a chip on is number 8, probability of success through luck is 1/36 digit 8 is played so left with 36 out of 37. One divided by 36 equals to 0.0277, it means chance of getting number 8 is far less than one out of 36 numbers, which is .0277, because all numbers have equal chance to win.  Never wait for lucks to be happening to you. Be proactive and start doing your efforts by taking one smart step one at a time. Those who wait for the luck to happen; don't take any smart step, don't narrow their focus & seek the truth, don't do any analysis of effort vs reward, do not take any initiative / no proactive move in them nor make themselves responsible, do not line up any activities nor remove distractions, do not do any continuous effort / compound effect and no acceleration, they just want something to drop from sky, in case of failure they blame to the bad luck in their lives.

There is no such word in life called Failure. If you keep on trying better than previous try, and focused with right measures adopted, you can never fail. You can only quit from trying. There is a hell of a difference between Failure & Quitting. The purpose of 80/20 effect is to see effort vs reward, so that no one quit, how much comfort can be sacrificed so that you do not think of quitting? It is an early test or working, estimation of effort you can perform according to your situation, so that at later stage you do not say ……. Ahhhhh; it is more than your capability or limits.

To be top achiever; be neither an optimist nor a pessimist but with a realistic check on its merits & demerits is an actual rational working, definite safety prevails or minimum damage if any unforeseen scenario erupts. Success nailers take numerous decisions every day, they follow 6 steps so fast that looks like no working done but they have fast speed, their radar surveillance working is fast.

Don't delay, grab the opportunity, work on it according to the previous 6 steps explained, you will win; you will become top achiever in any area of life you apply on these principles. Attitude also has a lot to do with success. Right attitude make you reach there easily. Build up success one after another, make it your habit, your entire life will become full of success stories; the way you spend your time collectively becomes your life, and every one's life. Over all collectively it becomes a healthy society.

Life is full of good and bad experiences, learn from bad times and look for good experiences all the time, your life will blossom, cherish and shine like a moon. People around you will feel the fresh breeze, and will love to be in your company, they will spread your words, your experiences; this is the success. Making money is not only the success.

Since the selfi (picture) has become so popular; people make selfi even on very dangerous spots and die as I mentioned earlier recently on mount Everest; Donald Lynn age 55 slipped from top and could not celebrate his success while taking selfi, why he could not celebrate his success? He lost his focus. This could have been his best life time success standing on top of Mount Everest. He forgot one of the six keys to success is keeping on focus.

Sometime small proactive moves become life time memories, I look back when I was on tour to Disney Land in 1999, I tried something unique with the normal traditional non-digital camera, turning it to facing myself and taken a shot. Now I believe in 1999 when no one knew what selfi was, I had experienced it 20 years ago a "selfi" sitting on a boat going into cave, I remember turning back my cap for a clear selfi. I feel proud and happy that may be I have been the inventor of selfi? So make your life full of quality good experiences by being proactive, which travel with you throughout your life.

Selfi: of myself taken in 1999 by me with non-digital camera in Disney-Land.

"If you go to work on your Goals, your Goals will go to work on you. If you go to work on your Plan, your Plan will go to work on you. Whatever Good things we build, end up building us".

-Jim Rohn-(65)

John Goddard, an adventurer at his teen age of fifteen sat down one day and listed down 127 different goals he wanted to accomplish in his life time, few of them were; explore 8 of the major rivers including amazon, climb sixteen of the highest mountains including mount Everest, fly and navigate around the globe, which he did four times, visit north and south poles, play flute and violin, study primitive cultures in dozen countries, read Bible start to end, by the time he turned fifty he completed more than his

100 goals out of 127 made at age fifteen. When asked reason of creating such fascinating list? He replied first; I did not liked to be told do this and do that, secondly I did not want to turn fifty and realized had not accomplished anything (66). Think big in life, life has lot to offer, why don't you enjoy your fair amount of share? Step up & dig deep where new ideas lie waiting for you to un-cover them by taking one smart step at a time and give them life and the life you deserve.

World is full of passionate people who set themselves for new records and inspire others too, even try more unique and innovative ideas;

During my school studies mid & late 80's, we read about man will fly in future, since then I have been looking into new developments, every attempt, every news, my that long journey of waiting is over until recently on 04th Aug 2019; Frenchman Franky Zapata has become the first person to cross the English Channel on a jet-powered fly-board. Powered by a kerosene-filled backpack, the inventor made the 35.4-km journey in 22 minutes (67). He was failed in his previous attempt in July 2019. He was forced to abandon a previous bid after failing to land on a refueling platform and falling into the sea. Eventually human dream to fly got fulfilled. I am glad I saw it in my life of man flying. This dream of "man can fly" could have been since human stepped on this planet. Different people worked on different ideas since then. It became possible of taking smart steps one by one then kept looking through research and development ways to improve, made different experiments, learnt again, narrowed down focus again, made new solution, checked its effects, tried again, focused on new learning and developments made it possible because different activities worked-out have been lined up to make it happen, compound effect made it possible because long persistence and consistency provided the results, people did not gave up. All those who contributed in this success have been very proactive.

It is beginning. More developments we will see in coming future. This development worked same way as aviation industry, when two brothers made first plane almost a century ago and now we have state of the art different planes for different purposes like cargo carrying tons of goods, fighter planes, and commercial planes carrying five hundred plus passengers. We by taking next smart choices see soon policemen flying towards catching criminals rather than driving in streets putting other people lives on risk. Flying crew can be an emergency doctor to provide first aids in few minutes, faster services as compare to ambulance running around in streets sometimes stuck in traffic. This success has no limits from now on.

Flying image of a Policeman carrying gun

It is evident success is not simultaneous, it has been long working behind this achievement, and it has not become possible through luck, it has been a constant thrive of smart moves, focused, motivation, lined up of activities, persistence to make it happen. Before this; adventurist are being jump from plane in sky with parachute or wearing swing suits and jump from hill. It had limitations of going downward only. But with this new development upward, left & right flying is possible.

Another land mark achievement on same English Channel recently; A woman in fact a Super Human "Sarah Thomas" aged 37; who was treated for breast cancer a year ago has become the first person to swim across the English Channel four times non-stop 54 hours swim on 17 September 2019, unbelievable. Can we do it right now? Impossible!!! How she did it? Any luck made her successful? No. She worked for it; she was all alone being Proactive & 100% responsible in achieving this target. She has been focused and determined, persistent as I explained compound effect has huge impact and it is proven to be a new world record of 54 hours nonstop swim twice UK to France. My head shakes when i think of it. Could she do it without being physically fit? No, for any single activity we must take care of our body. This is why to be a proactive life is basics to nail your success, right nutrient food is very important explained earlier. She built stamina like running a marathon race gradually, compound effect produced the results.

Ms. Thomas - who completed her treatment in 2018, dedicated her swim to "all the survivors out there".

It should have been a total distance of about 129 km but the tidal pulls in the Channel increased the distance by more than 60%, meaning she ended up swimming nearly 209 km. she was stung in face by jelly fish and described tough to deal with salty water hurting her throat but she did not get distracted. Great focus and persistency she had. I travelled twice from Dover to Kelly, once on cruise ship second under the sea on euro star train, I can imagine how scary is to swim 54 hours non-stop. This is Top swim marathon from this planet ever. To keep the body Nutrient and fit, Ms. Thomas relied on a protein recovery drink mixed with electrolytes and a little bit of caffeine to help offset sleepiness (68). This planet has immense & un-imaginable potential for those who want to "nail their success". Simply be healthy informative and;

Take small smart step one at a time

Take step by narrowing down your focus & seek the truth

Calculate how much effort you can spend vs reward 80/20

Be proactive and 100% responsible of whatever you do

Unfold objects with line up activities & remove distractions

Work with persistency keep in mind compound effect

Success is guaranteed, Become "TOP ACHIEVER"

*

"Actions Have Consequences, Efforts Definitely Contribute"

*

"Never Mind if you are Not Born as King, Live as King by

Nail Your Success"


REFERENCES

**Introduction**

1; 14 October 2016  Johanna Li Inside Edition
 https://news.yahoo.com/fearless-granny-celebrates-95th-birthday-190400127.html


**Chapter 1**

1; Max Tegmark page book life 3.0 Artificial intelligence page 26
2; Max Tegmark page book life 3.0 Artificial intelligence page 72,73
3; Ericsson archive, Wikipedia. https://www.ericsson.com/en/about-us/history
4;https://airandspace.si.edu/exhibitions/wright-brothers/online/fly/1903/
5"Commercial Aircraft Airbus and Emirates reach agreement on A380 fleet, sign new widebody orders" (Press release). Airbus. 14 February 2019.
6;  https://spacenews.com/stratolaunch-plane-makes-first-flight/   Wikipedia
Stratolaunch becomes world's largest aircraft to fly". Flightglobal. April 13, 2019
7; the one thing book page 87 Gary keller and jay papasan.
8; guardian 4 april 2019
https://www.theguardian.com/technology/2019/apr/04/jeff-bezos-mackenzie-amazon-divorce-deal-control
9; Pinker, Steven (1997), *How the Mind Works*, New York: W. W. Norton & Company p. 342
10; Muggeridge (1971), chapter 3, "Mother Teresa Speaks", pp. 105, 113


**Chapter 2**

1; Canright, Shelley. "NASA's Great Observatories". NASA. Retrieved April 26, 2008.

https://www.nasa.gov/audience/forstudents/postsecondary/features/F_NASA_Great_Obs ervatories_PS.html
2; the intelligent investor by Benjamin Graham revised edition page 21, 22.
3; By Brandon Griggs, CNN
July 29, 2011 -- Updated 1603 GMT (0003 HKT) | Filed under: Innovation
TECH; NEWSPULSE
http://edition.cnn.com/2011/TECH/innovation/07/29/apple.cash.government/
4; THE ONE THING by Gary Keller with  Jay Papasan page 192
5; The world's first ski descent of K2,  By Rory Smith, CNN Updated 1539 GMT (2339 HKT)
July 24, 2018
https://edition.cnn.com/2018/07/23/sport/k2-andrzej-bargiel-ski-descent-intl/index.html
6: Ericsson archive,  https://www.thelocal.se/20090625/20260
David Landes  david.landes@thelocal.com  @davelandes, 25 June 2009  07:37 CEST+02:00

<u>Chapter 3</u>

1: Richard Koch The 80/20 principle book page 4.
2: Richard Koch The 80/20 principle book page 6.
3: Gröndahl, Mika; McCann, Allison; Glanz, James; Migliozzi, Blacki; Syam, Umi (December 26, 2018). "In 12 Minutes, Everything Went Wrong". The New York Times.
4: "Ethiopian Airlines: 'No survivors' on crashed Boeing 737". BBC News. March 10, 2019. Retrieved March 10, 2019.
5; BBC 05 April 2019 https://www.bbc.com/news/world-africa-47553174
6; Jim Rohn quoted by Jack Canfield, Mark Victor Hansen, Les Hewitt author of "THE POWER OF FOCUS page 35

<u>Chapter 4</u>

1: *"Jack Ma". Forbes. Retrieved 11 March 2019. Wikipedia.com*
2: "Jahangir The Conquerer". emel.com. Retrieved 9 March 2016. Wickipedia.com
3; Poncha, Cyrus (15 November 2005). "Time Magazine Asian Hero: Jahangir Khan".

<u>Chapter 5</u>

1; (Daniel H Pink Book "When" page 25). Mareike B Wieth and Rose T Zacks "Time of day effects on problem solving: when the non-optimal is optimal", Thinking and Reasoning 17, no 4 (2011):387-401
2; (Daniel H Pink Book "When" page 25). Lynn Hasher, Rose T Zacks and Cynthia P May "inhibitory control, Circadian Arousal and Age" in Daniel Gopher and Asher Koriat, eds, Attention and Performance XVII: Cognitive Regulation of Performance: Institute of Theory and Application (Cambridge, MA: MIT Press, 1999, 653-675)
3; (Daniel H Pink Book "When" page 25). Mareike B Wieth and Rose T Zacks "Time of day effects on problem solving: when the non-optimal is optimal", Thinking and Reasoning 17, no 4 (2011):387-401

4; Mark R Rosekind et al, "Crew Factors in Flight Operations 9: Effects of Planned cockpit Rest on crew performance and alertness in long haul operations," NASA Technical reports server, 1994, available at http://ntrs.nasa.gov/search.jsp?R=19950006379

5; Tracey Leigh Signal et al, "Schedule napping as a countermeasure to sleepiness in air traffic controllers," journal of sleep research 18, no. 1 (2009): 11-19

6; Sergio Garbarino et al, "Professional shift work drivers who adopt prophylactic naps can reduce the risk of car accidents during night work," sleep 27, no. 7 (2004): 1295-1302

7; Felipe Beijamini et al, "after being challenged by a video game problem, sleep increase the chance to solve it," PloS ONE 9, no. 1 (2014): e84342.

8; Bryce A Mander et al, "wake deterioration and sleep restoration of human learning," current biology 21, no. 5 (2011): R183-184; Felipe Beijamini et al, "after being challenged by a video game problem, sleep increase the chance to solve it," PloS ONE 9, no. 1 (2014): e84342

9; Catherine E Milner & Kimberly A Cote, " benefits of napping in healthy adults: impact of nap length time of day, age and experience with napping," journal of sleep research 18, no. 2 (2009): 272-81; Scott S Campbell et al, "effects of a month long napping regimen in older individuals," journal of the American Geriatrics Society 59, no. 2 (2011): 224-32; Junxin Li et al, "afternoon napping and cognition in Chinese older adults: finding form the china health and retirement longitudinal study baseline assessment," journal of the American Geriatrics Society 65, no. 2 (2016): 373-80.

10; Nicholas Bakalar, "regular midday snoozes tied to a healthier heart," New York Times, February 13, 2007, reporting on Androniki Naska et al, Siesta in healthy adults and coronary morality in the general population," archive of internal medicine 167, no. 3 (2007): 296-301, cautionary note: the study showed a correlation between napping and the reduced risk of heart disease, not necessarily that napping caused the health benefit.

11; Brice Faraut et al, "napping reverses the salivary interleukin-6 and urinary norepinephrine changes induced by sleep restriction," journal of clinical endocrinology & metabolism 100, no. 3 (2015): E416-26.

12; Amber Brooks & Leon C Lack, "a brief afternoon nap following nocturnal sleep restriction: which nap duration is most recuperative? Sleep 29, no. 6 (2006): 831-40.

13; Jim Horne and Louise Reyner, "vehicle accidents related to sleep" A review; occupational & Environmental Medicine 56 no. 5 (1999): 289-94

14; Justin Caba, "Least productive time of the day determined to be 2:55 PM: what you can do to stay awake? Medical Daily, June 4, 2013 available at: http://www.medicaldaily.com/least-productive-time-day-officially-determined-be-255-pm-what-you-can-do-stay-awake-246495

15; Hans Henrik Sievertsen, Francesca Gino, and Marco Piovesan, "Cognitive Fatigue influences students' performance on standardized tests". Proceedings of the National academy of Sciences 113, no. 10 (2016): 2621-24.

## Chapter 6

1; Nick Mashiter (23 April 2017). "Mary Keitany sets new world record as she wins the women's elite race at the London Marathon". London Evening Standard. Retrieved 23 April 2017
2; "London Marathon 2017: Mary Keitany & Daniel Wanjiru win". BBC. 23 April 2017. Retrieved 23 April 2017
3; First Seven Years of Childhood: Are They the Most Important?
Medically reviewed by Karen Gill, MD, Specialty in pediatrics, on December 21, 2017 written by Juli Fraga, PsyD https://www.healthline.com/health/parenting/first-seven-years-of-childhood

## Chapter 7

1; Jim Rohn Quotes: https://www.brainyquote.com/quotes/jim_rohn_173313
2; Jack Canfield, Mark Victor Hansen, Les Hewitt. Author of; "The Power of Focus" p. 73
3; https://www.bbc.com/news/av/world-europe-49226353/man-crosses-english-channel-by-flyboard
4; https://www.bbc.com/news/uk-england-kent-49724851


Further References;


- Robert W Mitchell, The Awakening Word: Being called to the spiritual path. (Author; House, 2011) p. 62
- Matt Walker; Brain Scientist TED April 2019. Sleep is your Superpower
- PMBOK 4th Edition Project Management Book of Knowledge
- PSA: Gouma Egypt 22 April 2019 karim Gawad vs Omer Mosad
- The 8th Habit author Stephen R Covey; Book page 46
- Daniel H Pink Book "When" page 25
- Mark Twain, Mark Twain at your fingertips, ed. By Caroline Thomas Hamsberger, (Cloud, Inc, Beechhurst Press, Inc, New York, 1948), p 354 & Robert A Fiacco Author of book; Discover Your Treasure p, 89
- Quoting Calvin Coolidge: 'Press ON'," Staff & Guest Blog. PBS. May 24, 2011. http://www.pbs.org/wnet/tavissmiley/blog/staff-guest-blog/quoting-valvin-coolidge-'press-on'/] & Robert A Fiacco Author of book; Discover Your Treasure p, 96

9 789692 342605